PRODUCE FACTS
What Your Mother Maybe Didn't Tell You ©

Published by Comella Press, P.O. Box 80216, Portland, Oregon 97219

ISBN # 0-9646221-0-6

Pineapple Frank and The Fruit Cart logos are trademarks of Comella Greengrocers, Inc.

Author: Frank R. Comella, Portland, Ore.
Design/Edit: Joy Patterson, JP Publishing, Ptld, Ore.
Illustrations: Sara Wolfe, Columbia City, Ore.
Cover design: Susan O'Day, Portland, Ore.
Cover Photography by Bruce Benton, Portland, Ore.

10 9 8 7 6 5 4 3 2 1

Printed in the U.S.A.

PRODUCE FACTS

... What Your Mother Maybe Didn't Tell You!

By Frank R. Comella

A rule of thumb that Mother used to say is that if it grows under the ground, wash with cold water, start cooking with cold water and cover pot with a lid.

If it grows above ground, it grows in hot sun uncovered. So, start it in boiling water with no lid.

The greatest institution in the world is the human family.

TABLE OF CONTENTS

Introduction

Preface by Frank Comella

TABLE OF CONTENTS

TABLE OF CONTENTS

INTRODUCTION

by Joy Patterson

Many of those who shopped at Comella & Son & Daughter in Garden Home, Oregon knew Frank and loved him because he made us feel important and welcomed; and in our best interest, he taught us about produce. The Frank Comella experience was not only buying fresh fruits and vegetables, but also a lesson in the human spirit that Frank conveyed through his hand-printed price signs above the produce, reminiscent of the old Burma Shave roadway signs.

In 1990, I asked Frank to write a book so I could know what to do with a Kumquat (which I believed was one of those odd shaped roots he offered, so obviously no one needed this book more than I)! Four years later, after his retirement, he called and that was the beginning. I am honored that I have had this opportunity, and that Frank and Betty welcomed me into their home and lives. They will celebrate 50 years together in 1996 and they are such a delightful couple.

Frank says, as does Betty!, that he has saved everything and it is true, but all the memorbilia he kept has proven invaluable in writing his book. He has memory books filled with every letter he received from individuals, hospitals, corporations, and service organizations. His den has numerous plaques on the wall, as well as framed newspaper articles about

Frank. And his library is filled with reference books and video tapes of his local television appearances.

Frank Comella has been called "a champion for the produce industry;" "Portland's Prince of Produce," (he's embarrassed by the inference to royalty); and as the "Professor of Produce," bestowed upon him by THE PACKER publication which is one of the top publication and authority of the produce industry. He shared with me that his proudest moment was the full-spread article, dated January 27, 1990, in THE PACKER about Frank and Comellas and how the "...Professor of Produce promotes produce and educates his customers, as no other."

This book is everything I'd imagined and more. People of all ages will learn about produce from this warm, friendly, gracious man. Frank is quick with a smile, is truly humorous, and he cares. We felt his goodwill in the store and you will feel his goodwill in this book. There is so much information offered and you will probably read it from cover to cover. Consider this a one-sided conversation with Frank Comella, and if you have any questions... read it again and again! Thanks Frank.

"If you have the knowledge, let others light their candle by it."

PREFACE

People ask me why I have written this book. I wish all the questions were as easy to answer. I wrote this book for you, to share my seventy-plus years of knowledge of the produce industry.

Everything changes with the times, from car styles to fashion. Produce is no different. New advances in technology and a shrinking world have put an end to seasons like we remember. You can find raspberries in December and watermelons in January. Year around availability has made it even more important that you learn to buy with all of your senses including eyes, smell, and touch. But your responsibility doesn't end at the checkstand. By learning how to take are of your produce once you get home, you can be guaranteed the freshest, best tasting fruits and vegetables, no matter what season.

My early produce education was gleaned from following the "old timers" around the market and pestering them with questions. I feel it is my responsibility to pass on this legacy to the next generation by sharing this common sense approach to produce. You can learn a lot by reading a book, but nothing beats hands-on experience. If I can teach one person how to be more informed, I will consider my job well done.

I don't have enough paper to thank all the people who have shared their knowledge and encouragement with me over the years, but I'd like to try.

My family has always had our hands in produce in one form or another. To my brothers; Larry, Joe and Vince, my brother-in-law Don; my sisters, Madeline, Anne and Mary, thanks for believing in me.

To my wife Betty, my daughters Sandy and Cindy, and my son Steve, thank you for having faith enough to follow me blindly even when you questioned my sanity. You are the force behind me.

Joy Patterson, you made this book possible by listening to my stories, encouraging me to write this book, and translating my handwriting. Thank you.

Most of my book is about handling and respecting your produce, and these are my own opinions. May you learn to care and feel for produce as I do.

For all of the help they have shown me over the years, I'd like to thank the following in alphabetical order: Calavo Growers of California, California Artichoke Advisory Board, California Tree Fruit Commission, Del Monte Fresh Produce, Inc., Dole Tropical Fruit, Oregon-Washington-California Pear Bureau, Kwik Kopy's Brian O'Day, Sunkist Growers, Sunset Books, The Multnomah Village Post for printing my monthly articles, THE PACKER United Fresh Fruit & Vegetable Inc., Texas Sweet Citrus Inc., and Washington State Fruit Commission.

If there's a smile in your heart, your face will show it!

Happy New Year! May each new year see you happy, prosperous, and healthy! The new year is celebrated around the world at different times by various cultures with their highly diversified customs, beliefs, and superstitions.

One rite that many cultures share is the greeting of New Year's Day with horns, bells, and plenty of noise. This custom is believed to get rid of the evils of the old year and clear the air to give the new year a good start. I remember a New Year many years ago when I celebrated with my mother's pan and soup ladle. I put a few dents in the pan and my mother put a few dents in my behind! I don't think Mom approved of my choice of noisemakers.

January inevitably brings cold weather and virus colds that put us under the weather. Strange that we have put people in outer space but still don't have a cure for the common cold. The best way I know to keep healthy is to exercise, keep a good outlook on life, and eat right. Eating fresh fruits and vegetables is an easy and tasty way to get the vitamins we need.

Vitamin C is said to stave off the common cold. Luckily for us, it is found in its natural state in many fruits and vegetables. Did you know that cabbage, weight for weight, has as much vitamin C as an orange? What better way to get your daily dose than in a good pot of soup or stew. Grapefruit and tangerines are also full of vitamin C.

GRAPEFRUIT

The good news is that January and February brings out the best Texas and Florida grapefruit to help us fight against the sniffles. Grapefruit is so rich in vitamin C that one half of a medium sized grapefruit supplies 75 milligrams of vitamin C.

Today's superb grapefruits have come a long way from the original varieties. Grapefruit is a graft of the Pomelo which is the grand-daddy of present varieties. Before 1900 grapefruit were about the size of a baseball. In the mid-1800's they were called the "forbidden fruit." This was probably because they were hazardous to eat due to the long time-lapse and lack of refrigeration, from grower to market. With modern refrigeration, which we take for granted, grapefruit can be and is shipped all over the world.

In the 1980's, Texas had two very bad freezes that not only ruined the fruit, but killed the trees. In replanting, Texans developed the Red Rio Star, a grapefruit with a deep red interior that is very sweet and full of juice. In fact, it is the finest that Texas has produced. Try squeezing it for juice; it will be red and taste wonderful. Texas thinks so much of the grapefruit that it has been named their state fruit, proclaiming what the world has known for years: that the Texas Red Grapefruit is one of the reddest and sweetest grapefruit around!

The grapefruit season starts in October and reaches its peak of flavor in January and February. Now is the time to save money by buying your fruit by the case and sharing it with a friend. In selecting your grapefruit, go for the heaviest ones you can find. Since they are 90 percent water, you'll want them with some weight. Also check the firmness of the skin and inspect the shape of the fruit.

A wonderful way to start your morning is with a broiled grapefruit topped with a touch of brown sugar. Try a glass of squeezed grapefruit juice for your midmorning break, a grapefruit and orange salad for lunch, or

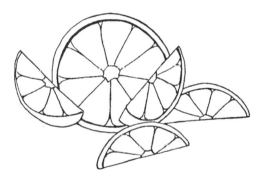

just slice one as you would an orange and nibble on it all day. If you prefer sugar on your grapefruit, try squeezing an orange on top instead! It will eliminate the acid and be sweeter. Remember, grapefruit is not just for breakfast anymore!

FRANK'S FACTS ON GRAPEFRUIT

Grapefruit juice poured over bananas will keep them white longer.

Grapefruit must be selected by weight, since they are 90 percenter water.

PAPAYAS

Are you looking for a special treat in the morning? Wake up and have a papaya. Papaya is the melon that grows on a tree. It is a fast-growing, branchless, tropical shrub or tree. The trunk is soft, almost herbaceous. Due to its fast growing from seed to fruit in one year, it raises the question of whether it is a tree or a giant perennial herb.

All parts of the tree are used except the roots. The milky latex of the unripe fruit, and other parts of the plant contain papain. The crude product is imported and purified to be used in food, leather, cosmetic, and drug manufacturing industries. It is used as a medicine for indigestion, and it is a natural meat tenderizer. Local Hawaiians use the papaya to keep their body regular!

The grower has no problems finding seeds to plant as there is 8,000 seeds to one pound. The grower will plant eight to ten seeds in every hole and then pull out the seedlings that are not doing well. It takes just one year from the time the seeds are planted to get fruit.

A papaya should be as yellow as possible. For a time, the papaya industry had big problems. It seemed that they could not use a chemical to kill the Med-Fly. They tried using a hot water bath of about 90 degrees for 40 minutes and about 102 degrees for 20 minutes. The heat caused the outside to turn yellow, but the inside was not ripe. Growers now steam the papayas to kill the Med-Fly. They use no chemicals and have done a good job.

When we were in Hawaii, it amazed me to go into a store and see papayas put into bins just like we have apples. I was tempted to buy a "plumbers helper" plunger which is what the locals use to pick papayas. With that you just reach up, twist it, and you have breakfast! A papaya that you eat in Hawaii is the same as eating a freshly picked apple in Hood River, Oregon — just wonderful.

As a very special treat, cut a papaya in half, scoop the seeds out and replace with lime sherbet, or squeeze fresh lemon or lime on the papaya. Mmmmmmm! The seeds of the papaya can be dried and then put into your blender, making a powder that can be used in your salad dressing.

The only time I got my fill of papayas was when we went around the big island of Hawaii and stopped at a fruit stand by the papaya groves. Big, ripe, sweet papayas were 5 for $1.00 so I bought five and gave the man a $2 tip. When we arrived at the hotel we discovered he had put 15 papayas in the bag. And we had only two days left to enjoy them! The maid must have wondered what we were doing.

FRANK'S FACTS ON PAPAYA

Papayas should be yellow as possible for ripeness. If it is still green, it can be ripened at 55-65 degrees F. in two to three days.

Never refrigerate an unripe papaya. A ripe one can be kept in the refrigerator up to a week, but don't set it directly on the refrigerator rack.

Papaya is a natural tenderizer.

Run the dried papaya seeds through a blender and add for flavoring on salad.

One half of papaya is only 80 calories and is loaded with vitamin C, folic acid, and potassium.

STARFRUIT

Starfruit grows where water is plentiful — Hawaii, Brazil, Africa, and now in Florida. It is also called Carambola (kah-rahm-BO-la). This oval-shaped fruit is 4-6 inches long with five deeply angled edges, or ribs which give the fruit the star shape when it is sliced. The skin is very tough, but the flesh is juicy and fragrant.

Early varieties bore sweet and tart fruit on the same tree. Now they have developed a sweet tree, and a sour tree. In picking out starfruit, figure that most tart varieties have very narrow ribs on the fruit, while the sweet varieties have thick, fleshy ribs. There are two varieties of white starfruit that are sweet. So, be sure to check your ribs... narrow is tart, thick and fleshy is sweet, white is sweet.

Buy the starfruit when it is completely yellow, or be sure to ripen the fruit for a few days at room temperature if the color is at all greenish.

A starfruit does not discolor, making it a natural for fruit slads or fruit cups. The skin is edible so the fruit does not need peeling.

UGLI FRUIT

Ugli Fruit is called ugli fruit because it is that. It has various, odd shapes and its skin is pot-marked. The only place it grows is Jamaica. It is a cross between a mandarin and pomelo. It peels very easily and has wonderful flavor. The only problem is by the time you learn to enjoy them, they are gone. Ugli fruit has a very short season.

EGGPLANT

Eggplant. Isn't that a chicken? Certainly not, and if you have never tried eating eggplant you are missing a true taste experience. An eggplant is a vegetable of 92 percent water, very few calories, and little fat.

To select a good quality eggplant, it should be firm, heavy, with a rich purple-black, uniform color. Avoid any that are shriveled or soft because they will have a bitter flavor.

Besides the large Italian eggplant, we are now getting the Chinese and Japanese eggplant. They are about the size of a small zucchini and have a lot fewer seeds than the larger eggplant. The slender Baby Japanese eggplant is sweeter than the larger variety.

Small eggplants are usually cooked whole. Larger ones are best in casseroles or for stuffing. Eggplant can be baked as you would squash, sauteed, grilled, used in stir-fry, or in casseroles. You can stuff it with your favorite stuffing; dice it and put in soup; bread it and deep fry.

Eggplant will brown quickly when cut, so place cut eggplant in a solution of 1 teaspoon of salt per pint of water. This delightful vegetable is available year around!

FRANK'S FACTS ON EGGPLANT

An eggplant should be firm, heavy, and a rich, purple-black, uniform color.

One teaspoon of salt per pint of water will help keep cut eggplant from browning so quickly.

Small eggplants are usually cooked whole. Larger ones are best used in casseroles or for stuffing.

Eggplant doesn't come from a chicken!

> You'd be surprised how you can win friends and influence people if you have some idea of what you're talking about.

FEBRUARY

February is the shortest month of the year, yet it offers many reasons to celebrate. February 14th is both Valentine's Day and Oregon's birthday since Oregon became a state on February 14, 1859! Although we celebrate Valentine's Day on the 14th, originally February 15th was set aside to honor the Roman god Lupercus. When Christianity became the official religion of Rome, the church merged the Roman holiday with the martyrdom of St. Valentine on February 14th.

POMELO

If you have a friend celebrating Chinese New Year, give your friend a pomelo with a tangerine (leaves attached) sitting on top. The mandarin on top is symbolic of better things in life, piled on top of good wishes. And by leaving the leaf of the mandarin on the fruit, it is a wish for fertility of land and family.

Giving the gift of a pomelo, is like a giving a four-leaf clover! You are saying, "May your house be full of joy, may you be blessed with many healthy children, may your land be fruitful and may you have a long life."

Pomelo literally means melon-apple. It looks like a tree melon and is the ancestor of the grapefruit. It is the largest of the citrus fruits. Pomelos range from the size of a grapefruit to nearly as large as a basketball, with some weighing up to 16 pounds.

The pomelo has a thick, soft pit and rind that is often used to make candied peel. Pomelos are sometimes called Shaddocks named for the captain who brought the seed to the West Indies in the 17th century. Pomelos are never bitter and are an excellent source of Vitamin C.

FRANK'S FACTS ON POMELOS

Pomelo means melon-apple. It is an ancestor of the grapefruit and is the largest citrus fruit.

Pomelos are sometimes called Shaddocks.

They are never bitter and are high in vitamin C.

PLANTAIN

The Plantain is a greenish looking banana with rough skins and a number of blemishes. It is an important food in all tropical countries. Sometimes, they are called cooking bananas or plantanos, but they should not be eaten raw. Plantain has green skin when ripe, and as it ripens further, the skin becomes yellow then black. Each stage of ripeness offers a different taste. They become sweeter as they ripen and when black in color they can be sauteed and served as a desert.

Use it as a substitute for a baked potato. They are excellent fried as a meat compliment, and when green they taste something like potatoes. Plantain can be one of the "like it or not" items, but try it boiled, fried, baked, mashed, sauteed, broiled, or deep fried, and then decide for yourself.

FRANK'S FACTS ON PLANTAIN

Plantain is an important food in all tropical countries.

Plantain is a greenish-looking banana but should not be eaten raw.

When cooked, each stage of ripeness offers a different taste; when green it tastes like potatoes; when black they can be sauteed as a desert.

WINTER MELON

Winter Melon is a large pumpkin-like melon with a frosty, greenish skin. It is most frequently cooked in a pork meat stock to make soup. Sometimes, the top is cut off and the soup is cooked inside the melon. Asians sometimes peel the rind and quick cook thin squares for a vegetable dish.

AVOCADOS

Have you ever eaten an alligator pear? I'll bet you have. It is known as the avocado. Avocados are very marketable in that they are not as temperamental as most other fruits.

Avocados never ripen on the tree. The tree, if fact, acts like a storehouse. The avocado can be held on the tree for months. Some growers leave their crops on the tree from November until May, harvesting them as they need to. The biggest problems a grower has is if there is a big storm or wind and the fruit is knocked off the tree. This is not a problem if the stem stays in place, but if the stem is gone it is necessary to drip some hot candle wax in the hole so the avocado will ripen just fine.

To test for ripeness while in the store, cradle the fruit in the palm of your hand. If it yields and is soft to the touch, it is ripe. Ripening can be advanced by placing the avocado in a brown paper bag or wrapping one in foil.

To tell if one is ripe at home, (not in the store) use a toothpick. On the stem end, pierce it with the toothpick and if it goes in easily it is ripe. If not, wait! Do not put unripe avocados in the refrigerator. To prevent darkening once they have been cut, brush with a little lemon juice.

Avocados are rich in fruit oil which is relatively unsaturated. For this reason, partial substitution of avocado for hard animal fats has been shown to have a favorable effect in reducing cholesterol. Avocados have no cholesterol. They have 11 vitamins and 17 minerals and 167 calories! Avocados are low in sodium and fit well in low sodium diets.

The biggest day of sale for the avocado is Cinco de Mayo (May 5th) which is Mexico's Independence Day. The second is Super Bowl Sunday. I guess guacamole dip goes well with football!

FRANK'S FACTS ON AVOCADOS

Avocados never ripen on the tree. If you have an unripe avocado without a stem, drip candle wax into the stem hole and the fruit will properly ripen.

It is best to buy avocados when they are green and ripen them at home.

Cradle the avocado in your hand to test for ripeness, if it yields to gentle pressure, it is ripe.

Place an unripe avocado in a brown paper bag or wrap one in foil to advance the ripening. Do not put unripe avocados in the refrigerator.

To prevent darkening of avocado once it's been cut, brush with lemon juice.

Avocados have no cholesterol. They have 11 vitamins, 17 minerals, 167 calories, and are low in sodium.

Try putting the avocado pit in your avocado dip. It will help keep the dip from turning brown.

If you can only use half of your avocado, put some lemon juice on the unused half, replace the pit and wrap. It will help keep it from turning brown.

You may use avocado on both your fruit and vegetable trays.

An avocado is also known as an alligator pear!

Experience is often what you get when you were expecting something else.

The best advice you'll get is from someone who made the same mistake himself.

To accomplish great things we must not only act, but also dream; not only plan, but also believe.

Many people suffer poor health, not because of what they eat, but from what is eating them.

March may "come in like a lion and go out like a lamb," but it is always time to enjoy spring vegetables and all leaf greens. Two of my favorites are asparagus and artichokes.

ASPARAGUS

Back in the days of trolley cars, the arrival of fresh asparagus (or as we call it, grass) was the first herald of spring. It came in March and bowed out in mid-July. Today, thanks to improved agricultural know-how, modern refrigeration, and the speed of the cargo jets, we have asparagus all year long.

The pioneers called asparagus "Sparrow Grass" or just grass. As they crossed the plains, they looked for wild asparagus. They knew they had food and water when they found it. Asparagus is the fifth most popular vegetable in the United States today.

It is a member of the Lily family which includes 120 species, but the garden asparagus is the only edible variety.

In Japan, Asparagus is cooked with sugar. In China, it is candied. In other areas of the world, it is used as a coffee substitute and a spirit is made from fermented berries.

Asparagus grows very rapidly, as much as 4 to 8 inches a day. When shopping for asparagus, look for two hallmarks that identify quality. First, is the condition of the tips. Look at the tops. They should be tight and green. Second, is the color of the spears. Turn it over. Do the ends show it has dry cells. Are the stalks green all the way down? Finally, aged and decayed grass emits a most unpleasant odor. If you have any doubts about asparagus freshness, let your nose be your guide.

The asparagus stalk should be as green as possible. When you get it home, remove the rubber bands. Lay it on the cutting board and cut off a half inch of the growing end. Wet a paper towel and wrap it around the stalk, half way up, then store it in your crisper or in a plastic bag in your refrigerator. Storing it this way will keep it green and fresh.

If the asparagus stalk is green on top and white on the bottom, cut off the white and run it through your blender. Freeze this and add it as a thickener to your

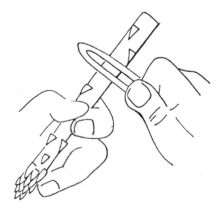

soups. Or, peel the white ends as you would a carrot, and add to your salads. This will help you use all of your asparagus purchase and save you money!

You can steam or microwave asparagus. Usually three to five minutes in the microwave on high is enough time to cook it al dente! The simplest thing to do with a platter of steaming, crisp-tender asparagus is to dress it with melted butter. Try using some in your omelette. Beyond that, there are a hundred ways to prepare this springtime delicacy.

March is the start of the California Asparagus. April and May are the biggest months of the Washington State growing season.

FRANK'S FACTS ON ASPARAGUS

Asparagus is the fifth most popular vegetable in the U.S. today.

Asparagus grows from 4-8 inches a day and was nicknamed "sparrow grass" by the pioneers.

Look for two hallmarks that identify quality: condition of the tips that should be tight and green; color of the spears which should be green all the way down.

Aged and decayed grass will emit an unpleasant odor so let your nose be your guide to selecting good asparagus.

Remove the rubber bands from the asparagus when you get home. Lay it on the cutting board, slice 1/2 inch from the growing end. Wet a paper towel and wrap around the stalks half way up. Store in your crisper or a plastic bag in the refrigerator.

Cook more than you need for one serving to have leftovers for salads and omelettes.

ARTICHOKE

Castroville, California is the Artichoke Capitol of the World. There were 12,000 acres of artichokes on the California coast in 1926 and today the acreage has changed very little.

The artichoke is a thistle. It is grown for the flower heads which are harvested before they bloom. March and April are the heaviest producing months.

Do you know who the first Artichoke Queen was? Read on and I'll give you the answer.

This springtime vegetable is known to many people who enjoy the delicate flavor and the smooth texture of the flesh. Artichokes have an unusual appearance. People who have never had one may see it and wonder what to do with it, or how to eat it.

To prepare an artichoke, rinse it in cold water and cut off the stem close to the base. Trim the thorn from the top of each leaf, if desired. Then cut about an inch off the top. You may steam or boil them. It usually takes about 30-45 minutes and when a leaf comes off easily, it is done. A piece of lemon in the water will keep the choke from darkening and adds to the flavor.

You may also microwave one by wrapping in plastic wrap. Be sure to leave a little water on the artichoke, and pierce the wrap. It usually takes 3-5 minutes, depending on the artichoke size and the power level of the microwave.

To eat the choke, simply pull off a leaf and pull the fleshy portion through your teeth. Some like to dip the leaves in melted butter or mayonnaise. I personally dip the leaf in salt.

After the leaves have been enjoyed, scrape out the fuzzy part of the choke at the base. Underneath lies the tender bottom. Just cut it into pieces and dip for wonderful eating.

Betty sometimes stuffs the artichoke. She cuts off the top of the artichoke. Then takes it to the faucet to run a strong stream of cold water in the leaves. This will open up an artichoke. Turn it upside down and drain the water. Using a spoon, she puts a dry mixture of bread crumbs mixed with parmesan cheese, in between the leaves and salt & pepper to taste. Then she dribbles some olive oil on top to keep the bread crumbs moist.

Finally, Betty wraps it in plastic, pokes a few holes and microwaves one artichoke for 5 to 8 minutes (depending on the power level of your microwave). The artichoke takes on the flavor of parmesan and gets so tender that I eat it all! There are many ways to enjoy the wonderful flavor of an artichoke.

The human heart can only be opened from the inside.

When people talk about artichoke hearts, crowns, or the marinated artichoke in the jar, they are not talking about someone pulling the leaves off of a big artichoke. These are immature chokes because when a choke is small, it has no thistle and the whole choke is used.

When buying artichokes, to test the freshness just rub two chokes together. If they are fresh, they will squeak. Oh yes, Marilyn Monroe was the first Artichoke Queen in 1949. For the record, she liked artichokes!

FRANK'S FACTS ON ARTICHOKES

Artichoke is a thistle. Artichoke plants produce year around, but the bulk of the crop is harvested between March and May. The fall crop peaks in October.

100 percent of all artichokes grown commercially in the U.S. are grown in California.

There are currently 34 artichoke ranches in California and nine shippers. Castroville grows 63 percent of all California artichokes. The artichoke is the official vegetable of Monterey County, California.

Artichoke hearts are immature artichokes that have not formed a thistle so all of it is eaten.

Artichokes will squeak if they are fresh. Rub two together.

Check stem of artichoke for any sign of bugs or decay.

Marilyn Monroe really did like artichokes!

CABBAGE

March brings us St. Patrick's Day and Corn Beef & Cabbage to celebrate the holiday. Cabbage is one of the best and most widely used vegetables — and like a good wife is often taken for granted. It is low in calories and ounce for ounce has as much vitamin C as an orange.

Cabbage was cultivated in ancient Greece and Rome and is one of the oldest vegetables known to man. From what I can see in some markets, they still have some of the original cabbages!

Beside the white cabbage, we have red, savoy, broccoli, brussel sprouts, kale, and cauliflower. Less common are flowering cabbages which originated in Japan. The savoy is a hardy cabbage with wrinkled leaves. It is very tender and does not take long to cook.

The main problem people have with cabbage is that they overcook it. When you can smell it you are overcooking it. To ease the smell, put some vinegar in the water, or better still drop an uncracked, whole walnut in the water while cooking it. This really works; it works with cauliflower, broccoli, and brussel sprouts!

I have found many people looking for large leafs of cabbage to make cabbage rolls. Anytime you have beautiful green cabbage, try freezing the leaves. When thawed, the leaves will be very pliable and make wonderful cabbage rolls. Try putting just what you need in a package for a meal when you freeze them.

Fermented cabbage leaves is called Sauerkraut. Sauerkraut on hot dogs is second to mustard on hot dogs in popularity. It seems that with sauerkraut, you either love it or hate it!

Try using Nappa Cabbage for a tender, flavorable salad. Nappa cabbage is used in Chinese cooking as stir fry. It also makes wonderful cole slaw.

Did you know the name salad comes from the Latin "sal" because salt was the only dressing used on greens. If tomatoes are too high for your budget, use red cabbage or radishes for color in your salads.

If you have lots of cabbage in your garden, pull it up roots and all before the first freeze. Hang it in a cool, dry place. Storing it upside down prevents the moisture from collecting on the leaves.

If you want to be the picture of health, you'd better have a happy frame of mind.

You can win more friends with your ears than with your mouth!

FRANK'S FACTS ON CABBAGE

Ounce for ounce, cabbage has as much vitamin C as an orange.

Don't overcook your cabbage. If you can smell it, you are overcooking it.

To ease the smell of cooked cabbage, put some vinegar in the water, or better still, drop a walnut still in the shell into the water.

Freeze cabbage leaves for later use with cabbage rolls.

Fermented cabbage leaves is called Sauerkraut.

BRUSSEL SPROUTS

These little cabbages were named because they were first cultivated in Brussels, Belgium. They cook fast in very little water. Make sure you cut a "x" in the bottom of the brussel sprout and it will cook in half the time.

Let the sprouts cook without a cover for five minutes, then cover and cook ten minutes or until tender. If the brussel sprouts are still on the stalk, be sure to remove them before cooking.

You can't sell the cow and still have the milk.

BROCCOLI

Broccoli, the word, means arm or branch. Broccoli has been around for 2,000 years and has been grown in the U.S. for around 200 years as a garden vegetable, not as a commercial vegetable.

In 1923, D'Arrigo Bros. started to grow broccoli commercially in northern California's Santa Clara Valley and in a short time they were shipping to New York's markets.

Please use all of the broccoli and not just the tops. The stalk is called Italian asparagus (by Italians!) and is very good to eat. To use the stalk, first peel it, then cut it in small length pieces so it will cook during the same time as the tops.

Broccoli can be found prepackaged in your market, which makes it easy if you want only the tops.

Ice is the best way to keep your broccoli for any length of time. As broccoli gets older, it turns yellow and smells so buy with your eyes and your nose. Remember to remove the bands as soon as you bring home your broccoli.

CAULIFLOWER

Cauliflower is available on the market all year, with a peak from August to October. Fresh cauliflower should have clean, white heads. In some countries, the green leaves are cooked like swiss chard or spinach.

Drop a slice of lemon in the water to keep it white while cooking. Raw or cooked, cauliflower is an excellent source of vitamin C, and one cup contains only 23-28 calories.

Cauliflower can be left whole or you may break off the flowerettes. The flowerettes cook between four to nine minutes in boiling water. But, please do not overcook or it will discolor. Don't forget the lemon.

To store your cauliflower properly, put it in a plastic bag and store in the refrigerator crisper. Keep the cauliflower dry, so don't wash it until you are ready to use it. Moisture causes cauliflower to go bad.

FRANK'S FACTS ON BROCCOLI & CAULIFLOWER

Ice is the best way to keep your broccoli for any length of time.

Remember to remove the bands from your broccoli as soon as you get home. It will help the broccoli keep its moisture.

A walnut in the shell will eliminate many of the odors caused from cooking broccoli and cauliflower, if it's thrown into the pot with the cooking vegetables.

Drop a slice of lemon in your cauliflower water to keep it white while cooking. Don't overcook it.

Store you cauliflower in a plastic bag and keep in the refrigerator crisper. Moisture will cause it to go bad so don't wash it until just before you're ready to use.

Try deep-frying cauliflower after dipping it in breadcrumb and egg batter.

SUMMER SQUASH

Summer Squash is eaten when immature while the seeds are small and the skin is very tender. In picking out summer squash, make sure it has a shiny surface. A dull and shrivelling skin is a sign of old age.

Besides the green zucchini, we now have a yellow or Golden Zucchini. A new squash on the block is the Sunburst which looks like a patty pan squash. It is small, flat, has scalloped edges, and it resembles a daisy.

The old favorite, crooked neck yellow squash, now can be found as a yellow straight neck squash. These are all called summer squash, but due to supplies from Mexico and Florida, we have summer squash all year long.

The person who looks up to God rarely looks down at people.

For a real treat, enjoy the squash blossoms. The large, gold, trumpet-shaped blossoms are delicious cooked al dente! Try steaming them.

DANDELION GREENS

How well I remember these. I used to wait for spring just so I could enjoy them. When I was a child in the 1920's, they grew wild in vacant lots. We didn't worry about pesticides then because we didn't have to.

Today, dandelion greens are cultivated and commercially grown. The dandelion greens I knew are gone. We spray our lawns to kill them. We live in a different era now.

The dandelion greens of my youth made wonderful salads with a vinaigrette dressing. The greens taste like spinach when cooked. The dandelion of today has large, partially toothed leaves which are thick and dark green colored.

Dandelion greens are extremely high in vitamin A. When you get them home, wash in salt water to eliminate any sand or dirt. Then wash them again in clear water and shake the excess water. Store the dandelion greens in a plastic bag in the refrigerator crisper.

Most of us like a person who comes right out and says what he thinks — especially when he thinks like we do.

LEEKS

Leeks resemble a greatly overgrown onion, but has a taste of its own. It can be broiled, braised, pureed, or stewed. To clean the leeks, cut off both ends and split them lengthwise. Run them under the faucet to wash out the dirt and sand, shake away the excess water and store in a plastic bag in the refrigerator crisper.

The leek is the national emblem of Wales because in 640-AD, during the battle between the Saxons and the Welsh, Saint David instructed the Welsh to put a leek in their caps. The Welsh won a big victory. Today, Welsh people traditionally wear a leek on their hat on March 1st to commemorate that victory.

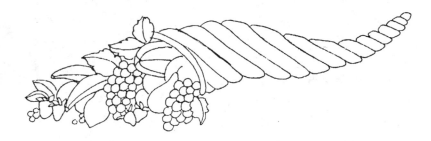

In honor of St. Patrick's Day on March 17th, why don't you plant a potato in your yard for good luck. I plant mine with my flowers. It's a tradition at our house. I am amazed how many pounds of potatoes we get from one plant. Happy St. Paddy's Day one and all!

APRIL

April will begin to see the end of the Navel Oranges and the start of the Valencia Oranges.

ORANGES

The Valencia is the summer orange — very sweet with a few seeds but wonderful for juice. Juice will not separate when squeezed ahead of time. Valencia is King of the Juice Oranges from California.

The Texas Orange is available from September to May. It is an unusually sweet, juicy orange. The Texas orange has some seeds, but a glass of juice will convince you how good they are.

When buying oranges, weight is how you tell a good one. Heavy oranges will have more juice. A green tinge on a Valencia orange is caused by the chlorophyll returning to the skin. It is just as ripe as an orange orange. It is called summer green, or regreening.

Years ago the Florida orange did not have the deep orange color that people liked and the oranges were colored with a harmless dye. This practice has been stopped. People like natural color and after all you don't buy the orange for its outside — but rather for the sweetness inside.

All oranges are required by law to be picked mature. As we know, citrus fruits do not ripen after being picked.

Due to the weather, California oranges have a thicker rind than Florida oranges. Florida and California produce over 85 percent of all oranges grown in the U.S. Believe me Florida oranges are very sweet. The Hamlin, Pineapple, and Parson Brown are a fine example of good Florida oranges.

FRANK'S FACTS ON ORANGES

Valencia oranges can be squeezed ahead of time. The juice will not separate.

Heavy oranges have more juice.

Oranges do not ripen after they are picked.

Green tinge on an orange is chlorophyll returning to the skin. It doesn't mean it is not ripe.

KUMQUAT

Did you know that the Kumquat is the smallest citrus fruit we have? It is grown in California and Florida and is available from December to May.

Kumquat is a tiny golden-orange fruit and is grown on a small, evergreen shrub. You can eat the whole kumquat and it doesn't need to be peeled.

You can add Kumquat to fruit salads, use in a fresh fruit drink, in desserts, and is very popular in marmalades. Kumquats have less than 15 calories each!

Store your kumquats in the refrigerator, with the stems intact and they'll keep for nearly a month.

PEARS

Now is the time to can and enjoy the bountiful crop of pears that we have in the Northwest. April, May, and June are good months for this.

Did you know that Washington, Oregon, and California usually produce 95 percent of the U.S. pear crop because of their ideal climate? Now you do!

The Bartlett is the only pear that you will find commercially dried. It is a summer pear and tastes wonderful, as well as being good for you. The yellow and red Bartlett varieties are smooth and juicy, the best of the summer variety for eating out of hand.

Pears ripen from the inside out, so place them in a paper bag until they yield to gentle pressure at the top or stem end.

Pears are called butter fruit because of the texture of the flesh. And they are called "Mid-ship" butter because the sailors would make pear butter that they would put on their bread, when the butter supply ran out.

Another reason you can't take it with you — it goes before you do.

MANGOES

Mangoes are sold in more parts of the world than apples. In India, which is the number one producer of Mangoes, they produce 7 million tons. That's a lot of fruit for a year. Akbar the Mughal, emperor who reigned in northern India from 1556 to 1605, planted an orchard of a hundred thousand mango trees. A mango grove was presented to Buddha which shows how important the mango is to India.

The Portuguese are given the credit for bringing the mango to the United States. A team of horticulturists in Lake Worth, Florida developed strains of mangoes that would grow in that state. The Hayden, Keitl, and Tommy Adkins are varieties all named for the grower. Mexico and some U.S. states are now using that root stock for their own plantings.

A mango tree is a big tree sometimes growing to heights of 80 to 100 feet. With the new dwarf tree stock, the size of the tree has been shortened.

When the mango is young and green it is used as we would use a zucchini. You may boil it, strain it, mix it with milk and sugar to make a custard. When the fruit is ripe, it makes wonderful chutney.

To select a ripe mango, you cradle it in your hand and if it has a little give it is ready. You can smell the end and it will have a nice flavorable smell. The mango pit, which is large, goes from blossom to stem vertically.

An easy way to cut your mango! Lay it on the cutting board and cut down on each side of the pit from blossom to stem.

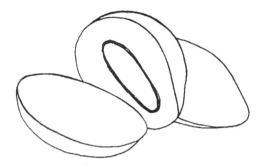

Now we have three pieces. Take one side piece and with your knife, play tick-tat-toe through the fruit, but be careful not to go through the skin when scoring it.

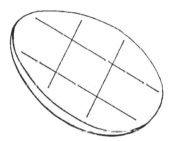

Holding the side in your hand, grab the outside of the mango and twist up — the fruit pops up. Now you can eat the fruit, or cut into bitesize pieces.

The mango has the flavor of peaches — bananas — even apricot.

There are people who can eat a mango, but cannot touch the skin. It makes them break out if they do. The mango is a cousin to poison ivy.

FRANK'S FACT ON MANGOES

India produces 7 million tons of mangoes per year.

If a mango is green, the pit hasn't formed and can be made into curries.

Ripe mangoes make wonderful chutney.

Mango is a cousin to poison ivy and the skin is an irritant to some people.

To select a ripe mango, cradle it in your hand and if it has a little give, it is ready.

Mangoes do not lose their color when cut. Try some in your fruit salad or milkshake.

The only person who got all of his work done by Friday is Robinson Crusoe!

PARSLEY

Since parsley is so full of nutrients, it's a shame more people don't eat it instead of viewing it as just a decoration. Italian parsley has leaves that are flat, bright green, and it is a little stronger in flavor than regular parsley that has curled leaves.

Chinese parsley and Mexican parsley all go by the name Cilantro. It is used in Asian and Mexican cooking. Use a sprig of regular parsley after eating onion and the parsley will remove the smell of onions and helps prevent the aftertaste, too.

To keep parsley from becoming limp on you, remove the rubber band, cut off 1/2 inch from the bottom, take to sink and wash it, shake out the excess water and put it in a covered, glass jar in your refrigerator. It may also be dried in your microwave to use later.

STRING BEANS

String Beans or green beans should be firm and fresh when you buy them. Put them in a plastic bag and keep them cool in the crisper. Don't wash them until you are ready to use them.

If you have string beans in your garden, pick them when they have reached about 3 inches long and pick them often. The more you pick, the longer the plant will yield beans.

When cooking fresh string beans, boil them until they are just firm. Don't overcook or they'll be mushy. After they're cooked, I like to add olive oil like my Mother did. Betty grew up on a farm and her family always added butter to their beans.

In the 1920's and 30's, green beans had a string along the top of the bean. It was a joy of love to have fresh beans to string. We would take one end off and run it down the bean to remove the string and get the beans ready to cook. Today's string beans have no strings. Modern technology has taken care of that.

String beans are an excellent source of vitamin A and potassium. A three to four ounce serving has just over 25 calories.

LONG BEAN OR ASPARAGUS BEAN

This bean reaches a length of 18 to 24 inches. People ask me why they are so long, so I joke with them and tell them that my son Steve and I had a hold on each end and just pulled them to that length.

Seriously, this bean is used in oriental cooking and has a flavor similar to asparagus. Buy long beans with your eyes. Check for freshness.

Keep your supply in a plastic bag and refrigerate the beans until ready to use.

FAVA BEANS

The Fava Bean is called the Broad Bean in England. It was a bean of my childhood. We called it the horse bean. It originated in North Africa and it belongs to the pea family. It looks like a large lima bean, but has a tough outer shell.

The fava bean grows well if planted in late summer or early fall. It needs long periods of cool weather. The plant will grow three to four feet high. When we were kids, it was the fava bean that we dried to store and eat during the winter. During the summer growing season, we would eat them fresh off the vine.

The dried fava bean can be stored easily and reconstituted with water at any time they are desired. Dried fava beans give flavor to soups.

Mother used to peel off the outside skin and put fava beans into her spaghetti sauce. It was always something I looked forward to have on top of my spaghetti pasta.

It surprises me that more people are not planting fava beans. Another tasty idea is to puree the soaked beans and eat them as a vegetable.

It was very easy to dry them on a piece of canvas. The beans grew in a pod that would dry and open in the sun, leaving the fava beans ready to gather. Then we put the dried beans in sacks and stored them in a dry place to keep all winter long.

BEAN SPROUTS

Bean Sprouts are grown from mung beans. Try to buy bean sprouts as fresh as possible. Take them home and wash in cold water, the colder the better. Drain off the water and leave the moisture on the sprouts to refrigerate.

It is best to store your sprouts in a glass bowl with a tight seal. A plastic bag will also work. Remember, sprouts grow in water so keep them moist. Enjoy your sprouts in salads, on sandwiches, or in stir-fry.

Remember what my mother always said...

"If it grows under the ground, wash with cold water, start cooking with cold water and cover pot with a lid.

If it grows above ground, it grows in hot sun uncovered. So, start it in boiling water with no lid."

STRAWBERRY

Now is the time to really start enjoying strawberries. Once they were available only in the spring, but now you can get them year around. Strawberries are a perennial of the rose family, and are an international fruit, growing wild in many parts of the world.

The wild strawberry, known as the wood strawberry, has almost disappeared in the United States. You can still find them growing along the Oregon coast line. They are real small, but long on flavor and fragrance.

The Native Americans were actually cultivating straw- berries when the Massachusetts settlers arrived. They called strawberries "writtahimneash," which they mixed with meal to make bread.

In the 17th and 18th centuries, the French took a small variety of American strawberry called The Vir- ginian, and a Chilean berry and developed the Pineapple Strawberry. In the 19th century, many more varieties were developed and these and their il- lustrious offspring are grown today.

In the last week in May, 1833, fresh strawberries were selling for $1.50 per quart in New York. In the same week, they fetched 12 cents per quart in Baltimore. The different pricing was caused by no regular rail- road service, everything was trucked in.

Before 1950, Oregon was the largest grower of straw- berries in the USA. Many of us remember the Marshall

Berry. It was sweet, juicy, and made the best jam. Unfortunately, it had no keeping power and the growers were unable to ship it any distance. So, canneries came from all over to process the Marshall berries for their jam products.

After 1950, California decided to grow strawberries. With ideal climate and growing conditions, Californians were soon growing more strawberries than any other place in the world. The Golden State now grows the largest percentage of the total U.S. crop. Strawberries are grown in every state, even Alaska. But in my opinion, when it comes to taste, the Oregon berry wins every time! They are ready to begin enjoying in late May to early June.

Strawberries are the only berries that keep their caps on when picked. This helps them retain their Vitamin C content. In fact, 10 large strawberries have 133 percent of the recommended daily dietary allowance.

If you have never been to a U-Pick Strawberry field, take the children out to a farm that has U-Pick berries. The first rule is to respect the farmer's field like it is your own. Strawberries are best picked in the early morning while they are cool. Children enjoy the adventure of picking and eating the berries. Make sure you take the proper containers to place the picked berries.

The best place to put your fresh picked berries is in the back seat of your car, not the trunk. The trunk is hot and the berries bounce around. You as the driver may get into the front seat, turn on the air conditioner to stay cool, while your berries may cook in the trunk. You could put an ice cooler in your truck for transporting your precious berry harvest.

If you don't have a cooler, make sure you put newspaper on the seat or floor below the berries. If you have to put them in the trunk, put an empty box on top of the berry box so the berries don't turn over and make jam. I found out the hard way.

The correct container for berries is the little basket that berries come in. If there was a better way to haul berries, the industry would do it.

Take your berries home and keep them cool until used. When preparing your strawberries, do not wash them until you are ready to use them. Then wash them with the caps on or the water will make the berry soft. Remove the caps after the berries are washed.

Almost everyone likes to eat strawberries. You can use them in the traditional strawberry shortcake, sundaes, pies, jams, or serve them plain with yogurt for a healthy treat. Whatever you do, enjoy them when they are in season!

A fool and his money is soon parted — the rest of us wait until we reach the shopping mall.

BLUEBERRIES & HUCKLEBERRIES

Blueberries are often confused with Huckleberries. How can you tell the difference? The blueberry will have tiny, soft seeds; the huckleberry will have ten or more hard seeds.

The huckleberry is one of the native fruits of the United States. In western Pennsylvania, they have a box huckleberry that is said to be the oldest living thing on earth (over 12,500 years old). That one berry plant covers several square miles. Imagine that!

The blueberry is cultivated by farmers and is a fun berry to pick. It is harvested from mid-April through September. We have many U-pick blueberry farms in the Willamette Valley. Be sure to pick with care, and respect the efforts of the farmer.

The blueberry and huckleberry can be frozen, and I suggest you freeze them in single serving bags without washing them first. Try washing them after you take them from the freezer. If you want to wash them first, be sure to freeze them on a cookie sheet and then bag them together so they won't freeze in a clump.

Enjoy your blueberries or huckleberries in muffins, pies, fruit salads, on cereal, or by themselves with cream. Mmmmmmm!

> The best thing to put into a homemade pie is your teeth!

FRANK'S FACTS ON BERRIES

Strawberries are the only berry that keeps its cap on when picked.

Don't wash your strawberries until ready for use. Leave on the caps for washing so the berry won't get soft.

The difference between blueberries and huckleberries is the blueberry has tiny, soft seeds and the huckleberry has ten or more hard seeds.

The huckleberry is one of the native fruits of the United States.

Check with the U.S. Forest Service for the best place to pick wild huckleberries.

Pick berries in the morning or when the berries are cool.

Have the correct container with you when you U-pick berries. The correct container is the berry hallock in which store-purchased berries are sold.

If you U-pick berries at a farm, eat only a few berries unless you wash them first.

Have an ice chest in the car to transport your berry treasures home. They will stay cool and safe from spillage.

Freeze blueberries in the summer to have all winter long.

Please respect the farmers berry farm when you go to U-Pick.

CHERRIES

They say that life is a bowl of cherries. Guess it means that life is sweet, beautiful, luscious, and sometimes it is just the pits!

Cherries were planted by the pilgrims in Massachusetts in 1629. In 1847, Seth Lewelling crossed the plains from Henry County, Iowa, bringing with him selected, grafted fruit trees. He transported the trees in boxes of soil which he hauled in a wagon drawn by oxen. The label of one of the cherry trees was lost, so the tree was renamed Royal Ann.

This same Seth Lewelling, of Milwaukie, Oregon was the originator of the Bing cherry. (No, it was not named after Bing Crosby). Lewelling named the Bing after his foreman who was a Chinese workman named Bing.

The Lambert cherry originated as a seedling beneath a Royal Ann tree in Oregon. It matures 10-20 days after the Bing cherries. The Royal Ann and the Rainier are both white cherries with a blush on the skin.

The marchino cherries we find in drinks are made from the Royal Ann. To me, the Rainier is the top of the line. It is believed to be a cross of the Bing and Royal Ann. The Rainier does not have the yield on the tree that the Bing does.

I will never forget the cherry tree that was in front of the house where I was born. I climbed all over that tree to get cherries before the birds. It didn't bother me if they ate half because I ate the other half. Today, it seems cherries have to be perfect for people to buy and eat.

One of my biggest peeves when I had the store was people eating cherries and then dropping the pits on the floor. The pit acted like a round marble that shoppers could slip on. So please, if you eat cherries in the store, put the pits in the right container. The market owner and the insurance company will thank you.

So, how do we store cherries once we get them home? Keep them in a plastic bag in the refrigerator for longer shelf life. Wash only what you need.

Remember, life is a bowl of cherries and it is only the pits if you throw them on the floor!

FRANK'S FACTS ON CHERRIES

Ten cherries have 44 calories, while a peach has 38 calories.

Wash only the cherries you are about to eat. Store the rest in a plastic bag in the refrigerator.

The Bing cherry was named for a chinese foreman named Bing, and not for Bing Crosby!

CORN

In the United States, the word corn refers to indian corn; the crop whose precise English name is maize. The word corn originally meant grain. In England, the word refers to wheat. Cornflowers are so called because they are common weeds found in wheat fields. In Scotland, a cornfield is a field of oats.

Maize is really a better name for the crop since it is similar to the common name for this crop in Germany and Spain. In the U.S., however, the more precise term of indian corn was long ago shortened to plain "corn." No matter what you call it, corn or maize, it's one of my favorite vegetables.

My father-in-law grew corn in the Washington state Yakima Valley for Del Monte. This was actually the beginning of the hybrid corn. It had no name, just a number that Del Monte was experimenting with. I often wondered what my father-in-law thought of me when I sat down and ate 10 ears of freshly picked corn at a sitting.

Air is the biggest enemy of corn. When the husks are torn away, the kernels begin to lose their sugar. We now have the super sweet corns that hold their sugar longer and stays fresh longer. We should thank the scientists who have developed a double gene sugar so that the corn has an extended period of prime quality.

With your homegrown corn, the texture and half of the sugar content is lost in the first 24 hours after picking in summer temperatures. It helps if you lower the pulp temperature with ice cold water, and then refrigeration to avoid the sugar loss.

Today we have not only yellow corn, but tri color and white corn, too. If you buy your corn from a farmer, farmer's market, or produce section take it home and take care of it. When you arrive home, if you are not going to use it right away, leave it in its husk. Put it into ice water to lower the pulp temperature of the corn. Then wrap it in a damp cloth and put it in the crisper or plastic bag and refrigerate. Use it as soon as possible.

Why not put an ice cooler in your car when you go to the farm or farmer's market. Put your vegetables and fruits in the cooler and if you have a stop on the way home, it won't matter.

Years ago, Mother used to put milk in the water to put moisture back into the kernel — today with the new varieties it is not necessary.

FRANK'S FACTS ON CORN

Air is the biggest enemy of fresh corn. The husk protects the kernels of corn within.

Lower the pulp temperature of your corn by putting it, husks and all, into ice water.

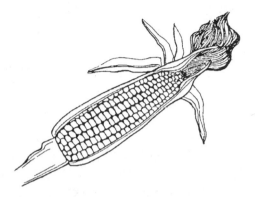

If you don't plan on eating your fresh corn right away, leave it in its husk. Lower the pulp temperature by wrapping it in a damp cloth and keep in the crisper or a plastic bag in the refrigerator.

The texture and half of the sugar content is lost in the first 24 hours after picking your homegrown, summertime corn. Lower the pulp temperature with the ice water method. Take a cooler with you if you plan to buy a lot of fresh corn from the farmer or market. It will transport home better and fresher.

Here's a hint, if you don't already know...don't put corn husks or silk in your garbage disposal. It will plug it.

Do you ever wonder why popcorn pops? The kernel has moisture and air in it and the dry heat causes it to explode.

> You know you are getting older when your knees buckle and your belt won't.

JUNE

You will notice the changes in your produce department this month. We have gone from apples, grapefruit and pears to the summer fruits: fresh local berries, peaches, plums, apricots, cherries, and a large variety of nectarines.

PEACHES

Peaches originated in China, where they first grew wild. Peaches moved along caravan routes to Persia and at one time were known as Persian Apples. The ancient Chinese cultivated the peach and considered the fruit to be a symbol of long life and immortality. In the late 1700's, Spanish missionaries brought peaches to California, but it wasn't until 1800 that peaches were grown commercially.

Christopher Columbus carried peach trees and seeds on his ship in 1493. Wherever Europeans settled, trees were planted; the French in Louisiana, the pilgrims in Massachusetts, the English in Jamestown.

Our freestone peaches were developed by a chance seedling planted in 1879. The Elberta was the first freestone peach. It came from Georgia. And now we know a Georgia Peach! The famous white flesh peach was also a product of chance. It was known by the name Belle of Georgia. For a wonderful peach to eat out of hand, try a Babcock, a white peach that will have you wanting more — more — more.

The hundreds of varieties can be divided into two groups, the Clingstone and the Freestone. The

Clingstone has a pit that is hard to remove, whereas the Freestone comes apart easily. As a rule, the first peaches of the season are cling, then come the semi-cling. The later fruit is Freestone. Today, we have many varieties of freestone peaches. Ask your produce man if you have any doubt if a peach is clingstone or freestone.

To ripen your fruit, put them in a brown paper bag. Do not fold the top over, but squeeze the center of the bag, leaving an opening. This lets out some of the ethylene gas and ripens the fruit with flavor. Keep your fruit out of the refrigerator until ripe, then refrigerate.

Most people prefer canning in late August or early September to get the best of the canning varieties. Every year, when I was growing up, my mother would buy 10 bushels of peaches. We would all help can them for winter.

Mother taught us how to easy it was to remove the skin by blanching them in boiling water for a few moments. She'd remove them from the hot water and we'd all peel peaches. The smells of peaches cooking stays in my mind to this day.

I remember Mother paying for her peaches with a five dollar bill and getting back change. We see a lot of people going back to canning, but not as many as I would like to see. We are getting spoiled by being able to get almost any kind of fruit all times of the year. I also believe many people do not have time to can or the room to store the dozens of canned preserves.

The peach's sunny color and sweet taste make it a delightful breakfast food. Sliced over cereal or diced into pancake batter, fresh peaches make breakfast special. For a dieter's lunch, try peaches and cottage cheese. Fresh fruit salad including juicy peaches is a cool and refreshing, light desert. How about peach cobbler, or peach shortcake.

Peaches are low in calories, low cholesterol, a good source of calcium, potassium, and vitamin A.

In selecting peaches or nectarines, look for a yellow, golden blush on the stem end. A little give on the top, not the side, tells me that the fruit is ripe and ready to eat.

FRANK'S FACTS ON PEACHES

Peaches and apricots originated in China and as people migrated they brought cuttings from their favorite trees.

There are two groups of peaches: clingstone, and freestone. The clingstone has a pit that is hard to remove, while the pit of the freestone comes out easily.

In choosing peaches or nectarines, look for a yellow, golden blush on the stem end. A little give on the top tells it is ripe.

To ripen peaches or nectarines, place in brown paper bag, squeezing the center of the bag while leaving an opening.

Blanch peaches for easy peeling by dipping them in boiling water for a few moments.

NECTARINES

What goes around, comes around and before World War II, the nectarine was green-skinned, white-fleshed, small and very good tasting. After World War II, the growers introduced new varieties causing skin color to deepen and change from a faint blush on a greenish background to the gold and crimson color.

The nectarine can be used in any recipe that calls for peaches. It has almost taken the place of peaches for eating out of hand. The white nectarine has been perfected and is a very sweet nectarine. If you get a chance to try one, do it and you will be surprised.

Learn to choose your nectarines as you would peaches. Often shoppers squeeze the sides of peaches and nectarines and buy soft fruit, not ripe fruit. The stem end must be soft to be ripe. When they are ripe, it will taste like the nectar of the gods.

How about a fruit cooler? In a blender, put 1/2 cup nectarine, 1/2 cup peaches, 1/4 cup sliced strawberries, 1/4 cup pineapple, and low fat yogurt. Add 3 ice cubes and blend until smooth. Now you have one large drink ready to quench your thirst.

APRICOTS

Apricots are available mostly in June and July. They are low in calories and high in fiber and nutrition. Select fruit that is orange-yellow and not greenish. It should be plump and fairly firm. To ripen an apricot, place in a closed paper bag at room temperature. Once the fruit is ripe, you may store it in the refrigerator.

If you plan to can apricots and buy a box, you can ripen a large group by removing the box lid and placing newspaper covering over the apricots to control the ethylene gases for ripening (don't replace the box lid).

Fresh apricots are a very seasonal commodity and are delicious in salads, jams, fruit desserts, and pies (Betty's favorite!). Just eat them out of hand because they are an excellent source of vitamin C and A, with only 18 calories.

PLUM OR PRUNES

Prunes or Plums — the best way I can explain the difference is that a prune is a variety which can be, and is normally dried without removal of the pit. Fresh prunes which are grown in the northwest are the Brooks, President, and Italian varieties. They are the European prunes.

Everyone looks forward to the arrival of summer fruit. Fresh plums are one of the special treats of the summer season. A fresh, ripe plum is the perfect snack. The Santa Rosa, Larado, Red Beaut, and Casselman are some of the varieties that Luther Burbank developed from the original Japanese plum. Luther Burbank enjoyed working with the plum. That is one reason we have so many different varieties.

Plums are best when the fruit is ripe. They should yield to slight pressure under your thumb. An unripe plum can be ripened in a bowl and should be softened at room temperature for a few days at home to bring out the full flavor.

Be aware that they ripen very quickly. Ripe plums should be used immediately or be refrigerated. Over-ripe plums can be pureed in the blender for uses in sauces. Fresh plum sauce over ice cream ... that's for me!

RASPBERRIES

Raspberries, like blackberries, are from the same family as the rose. Can you imagine sending some one a bunch of raspberries, instead of a dozen roses? If you could, they would be very happy to get them, I am sure.

When you pick a raspberry, the berry will separate from its core, while a blackberry core is part of the fruit. Remember that raspberries must be handled very carefully, especially if you are able to go to a farm to pick them. Please respect the property of the farmer and remember it has taken a lot of hard work to provide the berry plants and crop. To rinse raspberries, drop a few into a bowl of cold water. Don't wash the berry until you are ready to eat them.

Ninety percent of marketed, fresh red raspberries come from Oregon, Washington, and California. The peak of the season is June through early September.

The golden raspberry is a new variety which is available in a limited supply. It is yellow to gold in color and has a sweeter taste than the red raspberry. At one time, we had the black cap raspberry which was a berry that was used just for a dye. The dye was used to stamp meat with information from the meat packer.

FRANK'S FACTS ON BERRIES

When you pick a raspberry, the berry will separate from its core.

The blackberry core is part of the blackberry.

Don't wash the berries until you are ready to eat them.

Try picking berries early in the morning.

If you go to a farm for U-pick berries, please respect the farmers property.

Take the proper containers with you. Why don't you put an ice chest in your trunk for cool and safe transport of your treasure.

Check with your local highway department to ask about their spraying policies before you pick roadside blackberries.

BLACKBERRIES

As a child, we had wild blackberry bushes growing in open lots. We would wait until they were ripe and then pick them for blackberry tarts, pies, or just eating fresh.

As you may know, the really good berries were just out of our reach. Scratches, torn shirts and pants were common for us. We finally figured out that if we took a plank and threw it on top of the bushes, we could walk the plank to get our fill of big, juicy berries.

Blackberry supplies peak in June and July, but we still get some in August and September. You may see blackberries growing along the side of the road, but be careful in picking these as the highway department spray them.

Try picking your beautiful blackberries early in the morning. They will stay firmer longer. Today, we have many hybrids of the blackberry — Boysen, Logan, Cascade, to name a few. Whatever one you pick, enjoy them by making jam, jelly, or just freeze them for winter use.

> The human heart can only be opened from the inside.

FRANK'S FACTS ON FRUIT FLIES

One question that I am always asked is how to get rid of fruit flies. When you have fruit flies, you have over-ripe fruit.

If you have ripe fruit in the summer, put it in the refrigerator. Now wash out the bowl the fruit was in because the fruit fly multiplies in that juice.

A fan, or wind of some kind, will help also. Keep your fruit rotated, and if the fruit gets away from you and gets too ripe, put it in a blender and then freeze it into popsicles!

> The secret of good health is to eat onions.
> The trouble is to keep it a secret!

SUMMER SWEET ONIONS

When I was growing up (not out), people would say, "That man really knows his onions." It meant that they knew what they were talking about. Today there are many different varieties of dry onions, noted by the skin color, shape, and time of harvest.

Generally speaking, varieties that are marketed from February to August are sweeter in flavor. Those available from August to March are more pungent and excellent for flavoring. Fresh from spring through early summer, several growing areas now produce especially sweet varieties. These are referred to as Granex, or sweet summer onion and they begin arriving in March and end in August.

The first sweet onions come from Chile; then the Vidalia from Georgia; next the Maui Onion from Hawaii; and finally the Texas 1015Y Supersweet that was perfected by Texas A&M. Not only did they want a sweet onion, but one that made perfect onion rings. The 1015Y means that it is planted in the 10th month on the 15th day!

California, Oregon, and Idaho have a sweet onion, but Walla Walla, Washington has the Walla Walla Sweet Onion. Walla Walla is a town they liked so much they named it twice! The Walla Walla Sweet is available in July and August. You will have to be the judge of which one you like best.

In storing the early sweet onions, take an old pair of panty hose and put in an onion; tie a knot; then repeat the process until all are wrapped. If you hang them up and do not let them touch one another, they will keep for some time.

Don't store onions in the same place as potatoes because potatoes give off a gas that causes onions to sprout. Any onion can be made sweeter by peeling and placing in water for 15 minutes. This eliminates the sulfur.

In buying green onions that are bound with a twist-tie or rubber band, remove the band when you get the produce home. They will keep longer without the binding. Use all of the green onion — instead of throwing the tops away, use them in your stir-fry, salads, or on top of your fried rice.

Betty and I have frozen them, along with chives in our ice cube trays to use at a later date. Just fill the cubes leaving just enough room for some water to freeze them. After frozen, remove the cubes from the trays and put into a sturdy ziplock bag for easy access.

FRANK'S FACTS ON ONIONS

Store early sweet onions in an old pair of panty hose. Put in an onion, tie a knot; put in an onion, tie a knot; etc. Then hang them somewhere cool.

Don't store onions in the same place as potatoes because the potatoes will cause the onions to sprout.

Sweeten an onion by peeling and putting in water for 15 minutes. It eliminates the sulfur.

When you buy green onions, remove the twist-tie or rubber band when you get home.

Don't discard the green onion tops, use them in salads or stir-fry.

> A girl asked me out last week. I was in her house at the time!

Did you ever wonder what scallions are? Many of your cook books are from the east. In the eastern U.S. green onions are called scallions. For those of you in the east, you now know what to use when you read a western cook book recipe calling for green onions!

If scalding hot water is poured over an onion, it will not make your eyes water when the onion is peeled.

Hold an unlit wood match in your mouth (red end out) while peeling onions to keep your eyes from watering.

If your eyes are tearing, hold your hands under cold water for a few minutes.

Put the onion in the freezer for a few minutes before slicing and your eyes won't tear.

Put a slice of bread in your mouth when peeling onions and the smell won't bother you.

The heaviest thing a person can carry is a grudge.

Happiness is a healthy mental attitude, a grateful spirit, a clear conscience, and a heart full of love.

July, for me, is the month of picnics. With all the melons in season, we have a reason to celebrate. I go back in time when the biggest part of the picnic was the friends and relatives around you. then came the fried chicken and a big 30 pound watermelon.

Our Fourth of July picnic was always at the Oaks Park on the Willamette River. We would take the streetcar there to meet friends and family and the day-long picnic would begin.

The watermelon was taken down the bank and put into the river. In about four hours, we would go down and get it. My father would cut it open for all to enjoy. Spitting the seeds was always a game of great skill. Can you imagine trying to do that today?

WATERMELON

Watermelon is the only fruit you can drink, eat, and wash your face in at the same time! It is a native of Africa. In fact, Dr. Livingston is credited with finding the origin of watermelon. In Africa, as in many other parts of the world, the melon is not just used for food, but also as a source of water as it is 92 percent water.

If a person needed water for their livestock, he would break open a melon for them to drink. The seeds were taken all over the world by the slaves.

Years ago, when my son Steve and I were driving from Portland to Bend, we would stop at Maupin

Junction around 4:00 a.m. and put a watermelon in the creek. Around 7:00 p.m., on our way home, we would stop and eat it. It always tasted like nectar of the gods.

I've watched people pick out melons by thumping, slapping, and shaking. One person even used a straw like a divining rod to test the ripeness. I like a good solid sound when I choose a melon.

My brother, Vince, used to say if it sounded like when you pat your head, it was too green. If it sounded like patting your stomach — forget it — it was too ripe. If it sounded like patting your chest, it was just right. It works for me, maybe because I know the sound I'm looking for.

The fruit we used to know in the early 1940's and 50's have completely disappeared. The old varieties would crack and break easily. Many times, I put my fingernail in the end of a melon and it would split right down the center, so we would eat the heart of it. If you try that today, you would break your fingernail.

Today, we have many new varieties that are smaller and more convenient for the shopper. A good example is the Mickey Lee which is sweet, delicious, and about the size of a honeydew melon. We're now seeing the Texan-grown, yellow fleshed watermelon more often. The color of the meat may shock you, but the flavor is tantalizing.

The best way to buy a watermelon is buy it cut. That way you can see what you are buying. Make sure you check the price for value because markets have a way of charging more, but it shouldn't be twice as much.

Sometimes, the best buy is a full melon which you can share with your neighbor. My daughter, Sandra, takes the excess melon and puts it in the blender and freezes the juice in popsicle containers for the children.

The new seedless varieties are becoming more popular every year. Try them sometime and you may be surprised. The only problem with them I can see is that you can't spit the seeds through your teeth!

Watermelon isn't the only thirst quenching fruit, although it ties with the strawberry for having the highest percentage of water.

FRANK'S FACTS ON WATERMELON

The best way to buy watermelon is buy it cut so you can see what you're getting.

If you want a whole melon, listen for a good, solid sound when you're testing watermelon. Watermelon is 92 percent water.

Put leftover watermelon in a blender and then make popsicles for the kids.

THIRST QUENCHING FRUITS

So, if you are feeling thirsty, try one of these:

	Water content:
Watermelon	92%
Strawberry	92%
Peach	88%
Nectarine	86%
Blueberry	85%
Apple	84%
Grapefruit	81%
Sweet Cherries	81%
Grapes	81%
Banana	74%

CANTALOUPES

How do you choose a good, sweet, ripe cantaloupe? Squeeze it or smell it or shake it, all you get is exercise. After a cantaloupe is picked from the vine, you can't put flavor back into it. It contains no starch to keep adding flavor. It will ripen just fine, but the way it is picked is the way you get it.

Out in the field, the cantaloupe has a pulp temperature of 100-110 degrees F. It is picked and run through a hydro-cooler which drops the pulp temperature down to 32-35 degrees.

So you look at how it was picked. The slip end should be clean and should have an indentation. I call it an inside belly button. This tells me it was ripe when it was picked and will be full of flavor. If it has an outside belly button, it was picked green. Again, it will ripen but it will not have as much flavor.

If you cut your cantaloupe and only use half now, leave the seeds in the other half and wrap with clear plastic. Otherwise, the other items in your refrigerator will absorb the smell of the cantaloupe.

Try cutting your cantaloupe and other melons in quarters. You can get 20 to 30 nice cuts on a melon by cutting the quarters on the bias at a slant.

The word cantaloupe comes from the word "cantaluppi," the name of a former summer residence of the Pope near Rome, Italy.

HONEYDEW MELON

We all know about Honeydews. Yup honeydew this — honeydew that. A good, ripe honeydew melon is hard to beat, but a green honey dew is a waste of money. After a honeydew is cut, it will not ripen.

Honeydews should be purchased fully ripe with a creamy outer color and velvety feel to the surface. The flesh should be pale green. Ripeness may be indicated by smell and slight softening at the blossom end.

CRENSHAW MELON

To me, this is the King of the melons. The bright salmon flesh is sweet and firm. It is one melon you can smell the flavor. A little softening at the end also helps judge the ripeness. I love to sprinkle lemon on this melon!

SANTA CLAUS MELON

Santa Claus or Christmas melon was called this because it was the last melon of the season. Not anymore because we have no seasonal limits and they come from somewhere all the time. The santa claus resembles a small watermelon with a mottled yellow and green rind.

The pale green flesh tastes similar to honeydew. To test for ripeness, the rind should give slightly under light pressure.

Even the seed of any melon mentioned above serves a purpose. A great activity for children is to dry the seeds, string them into necklaces, and then paint the seeds. Dried watermelon seeds are eaten like nuts by Asians.

KIWIFRUIT

Have you ever eaten a chinese gooseberry? You are every time you enjoy a Kiwifruit. Chinese gooseberries were brought from New Zealand to the Los Angeles market. Not many people would buy them. The name was changed to Kiwifruit, shortened to Kiwi, and the rest is history.

A new fruit was born in the U.S. What was once considered strange, the little egg-shaped fruit with the suede-like covering has become popular in tarts or as a garnish. It is a beautiful sight with the emerald green kiwifruit and its starburst pattern of tiny black seeds.

We are lucky that we have Kiwi all year long; six months from New Zealand, and six months from California. We import April through September with the largest shipments coming in July. The California crop supplies us between December through June.

The Kiwi grows on a vine like grapes. I planted two Kiwi in my backyard. I have a beautiful vine, but no fruit. It takes two trees to grow Kiwi, but make sure

one of them is a pollinator. Looks like I need a pollinator in my backyard!

Oregon grows quite a lot of this fruit. Kiwi has a long
shelf life. After you buy or grow it, put it in the
refrigerator until ready to use. Then take it out and
use when it is soft to the touch as you cradle it like an
egg.

To ripen Kiwifruit, put in a brown paper bag with
banana peel or an apple. Both of these give off
ethylene gas to ripen fruit.

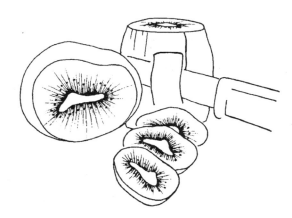

To cut Kiwi, cut off the top and bottom and peel the
suede-like covering down the sides. Slice and serve
on a fruit platter. Betty's favorite method is to cut the
Kiwi in half and just eat it with a spoon!

If you want to know how many friends you have,
just buy a cottage on a lake!

GRAPES

The oldest fruit plant cultivated by man is the grape. The U.S. produces more grapes than any other fruit, with the exception of apples and oranges.

The Concord grape, which has the slip skin, is one of the native fruits of the United States. Slip skin is a reference to the fact that the grape slips from the skin when squeezed. The Thompson seedless is an European variety. The first grapes we get for the year are from Chile and in the last few years Chile has really upgraded their product. This upgrade includes their peaches and nectarines, too. After all, it is summer in Chile when it is winter in the U.S.

Try to buy amber grapes for sweetness. A grape does not get any sweeter after it is picked. On one of my trips to California, I was talking to a grower of sweet potatoes, yams, and grapes. I asked him if I could have a bunch of grapes and he said yes. I took a yellow bunch off the vine, but I could only eat half of them because the sugar content was too much for me. After they are picked, the grape will not ripen anymore.

Years ago, growers used to spray the grapes to keep them from falling off the bunches. Today they can't do that. That is why grapes are in bags in the markets. I am proud to say that they, the growers, are not using a lot of chemicals and they should be commended.

As you know, the seedless grapes come in white, black, and red varieties 'now. The Flame seedless is large, crisp, and juicy. Grapes are filling and nutritious with only 107 calories in one cup. They contain vitamin C and potassium and are low in sodium.

This summer try freezing some grapes. Remove them from the stems, but twist them off rather than pull. Then you won't split the grape. If you wish to freeze a large amount to store in a single container, be sure to freeze them on a cookie sheet first so they won't stick together and then transfer the frozen grapes to the container.

Otherwise, you can put the unwashed grapes in a freezer bag, but I suggest you freeze them in a bag size that you can eat in one sitting. Then wash them before eating, if you want. Put them in a thermos to take on trips — very refreshing.

Many markets have loose grapes that have separated from the stem. Talk to your produce man about buying these, or ask that they be saved for you. And you will probably be able to buy them at a reduced price.

RAISINS

In 1873, a severe heat wave struck the California San Joaquin Valley, in September of that year. It shrivelled the grapes on the vine. One grower decided to harvest his accidental crop and took it to the market. A demand for raisins soon developed and a new American crop was born.

I had the privilege of being taken through a raisin plant in Del Ray, California. After all the grapes had been picked in the fall, there were hundreds of bins of drying grapes in the sheds. Thompson and Flame seedless made up the largest varieties used.

The brown raisins are dried in the sun. It used to be that they were put on grape boards, but this was hard because every time it rained, they were taken from the field and put in a shed. Now, they use parchment paper. If it starts to rain, they just roll it up, and leave it outside.

The old, weathered grape boards are now used by crafts persons for tole painting and decoupage. Betty has done some beautiful tole paintings on these grape boards.

The Golden raisin goes through a process of bleaching, but it is the same grape used for both the Dark and Golden raisin.

PEPPERS

BELL Peppers — green, golden, black, and red — are popular for their zesty flavor. The pepper is also famous as a salad vegetable. Sweet bell peppers will mature to various colors depending on the variety. The most common varieties of bell peppers will turn from green to red. As a green pepper matures, it turns red and is sweeter. Other varieties will turn gold or purple. The purple bell pepper will turn back to green when cooked.

Green peppers freeze very well. Just slice them and put them in the freezer. They won't be like fresh, but they'll be wonderful for cooking.

If you stuff a pepper, use a muffin tin to hold them while cooking. They will hold their shape better. Even better, instead of slicing the top from the pepper to stuff it, try cutting the pepper from top through to the bottom to make two halves for stuffing. They will cook faster and they are easier to eat.

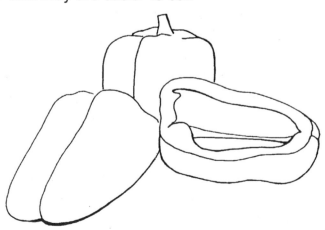

CHILI Peppers have been in great demand in the last few years, due in part to the Asian and Mexican population. Some varieties like the Anaheim chile and Pasilla chile are quite mild. Other varieties like Jalapeno and Serrano should be used sparingly when spicing dishes.

Let me explain the "Scolville Heat Unit" scale. The range of a pepper heat unit is between 500 to 400,000 units per Scolville. I would advise you to pay special attention to the heat unit category of the following chili peppers!

The heat unit of an Anaheim is between 1,000 and 1,500 and the heat unit of the Serrano is 7,000 to 25,000. Always be careful to avoid the seeds which is where your heat is. The hottest chile pepper was found growing in a field of peppers. It seems there was no market for hot peppers and the price paid to growers was so cheap that they decided to plow under their fields.

A grower decided to save some plants for his own use. They were different than those he was plowing under. That plant was the start of one of the hottest chili peppers in the world, namely the Habanero (Red Savina). Its heat unit is 300,000 to 400,000 which is 2,000 times hotter than a Jalapeno. Use the Habanero with discretion. Wear rubber gloves and wash all items used preparing it. A pair of tongs are useful.

A little of this pepper goes a long, long way. Learn to respect these hot peppers — don't rub your eyes. I have found that when I eat a hot pepper and burn my mouth, I can get relief with a spoonful of sugar. It absorbs it, while water just washes it down the throat. Some people drink milk to relieve the burning sensation.

To peel a chili, hold it over a flame or roast it. Put the heated chili in a paper bag for 15 minutes — the skins will come right off. Gloves are good to use when handling the skins. Hot chilies should not be handled by children.

The dried chili wreaths are called Ristras, which is a symbol of plenty and hope. Chilies originated in Latin America, where for centuries they have been used in flavoring and as a natural preservative.

GARLIC

Garlic has served many practical purposes other than as a remedy for illness. If you wear garlic on Halloween and it will protect you from demons and witches. The Greeks and Romans threw boiled garlic seeds on their fields to protect the young plants. Birds would eat the garlic seeds and fall asleep. Then they could be trapped and taken to other locations by the farmer.

Garlic was planted in rows by Dad. When the tops were dead, we would pick the garlic for drying. Many braids of garlic and tops were made by the downstairs stove. They were wonderful memories. Mother would fix Dad a bulb of garlic at every meal. Mother knew the medicinal value of garlic, I guess.

Garlic is a member of the lily family. The garlic bulb is made up of small cloves. To use garlic, break off a clove from the bulb and remove the outer skin. Then it can be chopped, sliced, or smashed by laying the clove on the cutting board and hitting the it with the side of a knife.

Once garlic is cooked, it has a nutty flavor. Store garlic in a cool, dry place. Move it around so it doesn't touch any other garlic to cause moisture.

> A man who eats garlic lives a long life, but a lonely life.

CANNING

Betty's rule of thumb — It takes two pounds of fruit to fill a quart.

In canning, most people want the fruit to be ready when they are. Unfortunately, it does not work that way. When the fruit is ready, make time to can or freeze it. Buy and can good fruit. It is a waste of money to throw away half of the fruit because of bruising. Use any over-ripe fruit in jams or jellies.

The only way to be sure how to process foods is to insure safety and nutritional goodness. You should refer to a recommended authoritative source of canning information. If you use sound, clean, raw product that is packed in sound, clean containers and subjected to the recommended heat processes the resulting food will be wholesome and safe.

There are new varieties of fruit and vegetables that must use new time and heat to end with a safe product. Check with your Extension Service. They will have the answers to your questions. Sometimes, what you did in canning in the past won't work this year (especially with tomatoes). It helps to say "thank you" to the Extension Service for their help.

STORAGE

A safe and inexpensive way for people to store vegetables for winter is a root cellar or a pit storage. Dad and I would dig a hole in a well-drained location under the eves of the house. As we had a lot of fruit and vegetables on the farm, we made it two feet deep by 30 inches wide. We put sand or gravel on the bottom of the pit for draining. On top of this, we put straw. We placed the vegetable or fruit on the straw and would cover with more straw. If you try this, make sure you keep below the freeze line in your area. You can put dirt or planks on the top of the hole. Put a pipe in the pit for ventilation so it extends a foot or so outside of the ground. Your extension agent has plans on root cellars. Again, if you have any questions, they are good people to ask.

SEPTEMBER

I know we've had a wonderful growing season because someone is leaving me zucchini in my mailbox! Now I like zucchini, but if you're going to leave them in my mailbox, at least put a stamp on them. I would guess the person leaving the zucchini bought a full flat of plants last spring. I hope they have learned to buy just three or four plants next year.

ZUCCHINI

My mother used to scoop out the seeds of a large zucchini and stuff it with rice and hamburger and bake it. What a treat. Zucchinis make delicious sweet bread, as well as batter-dipped, deep fried zucchini slices.

The word squash comes from the Indian word "askootasquash" which means "eaten green or raw." In Europe, if you asked for a squash they wouldn't know what you were talking about. There, it is more commonly called vegetable marrows or courquettes.

There are many varieties of summer squash, other than zucchini. Try yellow crooked-neck, yellow zucchini, patty pan, and scallipini squash to name a few.

WINTER SQUASH

Before the day of artichokes, asparagus, and other vegetables that are available year around, winter squash was in great demand. The HUBBARD squash — 20 to 40 pounds each — were huge by todays standard. These giants were cut into pieces and sold.

The seeds were roasted. Today, these large squash are losing ground in the markets to the DANISH (acorn) squash, GOLDEN NUGGET squash, and DELICATA SWEET DUMPLING squash to name a few that are all much smaller squash. Each are easy to bake just for one meal. Hubbard or any cut squash should be used as soon as possible.

SPAGHETTI SQUASH

Spaghetti squash or Vegetable spaghetti — no matter how you write it, it's a strange novelty. Spaghetti squash has a hard shell and you should make sure it is mature. Remember, the thumb nail trick: a thumb nail that goes into the winter squash too easily tells me that it is still green.

On the other hand, if the spaghetti squash is too hard to cut in half, cook it for awhile and then take it out and cut it. Be careful you do not get burned.

After it is baked, pull out the long fibers and you've got spaghetti! Cover with your favorite tomato sauce and enjoy. Spaghetti squash is a winter squash and keeps very well if curried.

CUCUMBERS

I like cucumbers with vine-ripened tomatoes and sweet onions with an Italian dressing. When cucumbers are small they are called pickling cukes. When they grow over four to five inches, they are called cucumbers.

"As cool as a cucumber" is an expression based on fact. The interior of the cucumber can be as much as twenty degrees cooler than the outside air on a warm day. Cucumbers have as much as 95.6 percent water.

Try peeling your cucumber and take a fork and run it down from end to end. The cuke will have a fringed edge. This makes a nice addition to your vegetable trays.

When you plan to make pickles, make sure you buy them as fresh as you can. My sister-in-law, Kate Eves, makes the best sweet pickles, the E.Z. way! Fill a scalded jar with small cukes. Add 1 tablespoon mixed spice, 1 tablespoon pickling salt, 1/2 teaspoon Alum, 1 cup vinegar, 1 teaspoon horseradish (optional). Fill jar with cold water and seal. Several days before you want to use them, open, wash pickles with cold water, and dump the brine. Clean the jar. Split the cukes, add 1 cup sugar, put lid back on the cleaned jar and place in the refrigerator. When sugar dissolves, the pickles are ready to eat. Shake the jar often to speed the process. This system is very easy and makes wonderful sweet pickles.

PEAS

Peas are an item you buy with your hands. They will squeak when you feel them. Peas are also one of the items that the frozen vegetable is as good as what you may buy in a market. That is, unless you grow your own! There is something special about peas that you pick fresh from the garden. They have a flavor all their own. I remember fresh peas and small young, new potatoes. What a treat. After removing the peas, I would also save the best pods and make PT boats. I'd wedge a little piece of wood between the sides and the pod would float in the bath tub.

Peas were first planted by Christopher Columbus in 1493. They were call pease then, but the name was shortened to peas in 1770.

SNOW PEAS or SUGAR PEAS have the edible pod and have been around since the 15th century. They were developed by the Dutch and are used in Chinese cooking, especially stir-fry. Store them in a plastic bag for longer shelf life. Keep them in your refrigerator and keep them dry. Wash them just before using.

SUGAR SNAP PEAS have been around for 16 years. They were developed by Calvin Lamboon in 1979. He was looking for a snow pea that would stay straight and not twist. The word snap comes from the fact that they can snap when broken in half. You don't see many fresh sugar snap peas in the market because they freeze so well and are shipped directly to the canneries, but production of the sugar snaps has increased so fresh snaps are becoming more available.

GREEN PEAS also called ENGLISH PEAS have a large pod that bulges away from the pea inside. The actual size of the pea can be determined only by the opening of the pod. Keep green peas in a plastic bag and store in the refrigerator, but don't get them wet.

They will mildew with too much water. Use green peas as soon as possible.

WINTER ONIONS

Winter onions are mild to hot and are called Grano. This late or main crop of onions is mostly of the globe type. Yellow globe is a commercial term applied to several varieties and strains.

The onion, amaryllis, and narcissus are members of the same family. The onion has been cultivated and known as an article of food from the earliest period of history. Onions were a food staple for the pyramid workers. Egyptians also used them as offerings to their gods.

The onion was introduced into the West Indies soon after their discovery. From there it soon spread to all parts of America. Onions were grown by the colonists and soon afterward by the Native American Indians.

One onion tale is that the juice annointed upon a bald head in the sun bringeth the hair again, very speedily. Believe me, it doesn't work. I tried it and all I got was onion juice all over. One thing I did discover is I smelled so bad that people thought I looked thinnner from a distance!

In 1864, General U.S. Grant said, "I will not move my army without onions." The next day three trainloads of onions were started toward the front.

The globe onion has better keeping quality that the Granex (sweet onion). It has quite a bit more flavor for cooking and stir-fry. Look hard for firm onions. Avoid onions that have wet or soft necks. Size has nothing to do with onion quality. Selection for size depends on the use to which the onions are to be put.

FRANK'S FACTS ON ONIONS

Yellow globe onion is a term applied to several varieties of winter onions, the late or main crop of onions.

An onion is 89 percent water. Look for a hard or firm onion. Avoid onions with wet or soft necks.

Store your onions away from potatoes as they will cause the onions to sprout.

Move your stored onions around in their bin each time you get one to use to prevent decaying.

Winter onions keep better than summer onions.

Rubbing an onion on a bald head will only make you look thinner!

> The human body, with proper care, will last a lifetime!

OCTOBER

Well, here it is October. This month we start to bid "good-bye" to summer fruit and say "hello" to a wonderful array of apples, pears, pumpkins and squash.

APPLES

October is National Apple Month. Most of the apples are picked and put into cold storage this month. Some go into common storage and others to controlled atmosphere storage, where the apple is put into hibernation. When put in a tightly sealed chamber and cooled to 31 degrees Fahrenheit, with 95 percent of the oxygen removed, apples essentially stop maturing. This is why we are getting apples all year long. When I was a child, apples would be gone by January. Today we have no apple seasons.

Apples have been a part of history since the beginning of time. Adam and Eve got involved over an apple. (I wonder if it was a Delicious?) Snow White had her share of apples from the wicked witch. How about William Tell shooting the apple off his boy's head? What a way to get a part in your hair!

Sir Isaac Newton discovered universal gravitation by the fall of an apple in the garden at Woolsthorpe. And let's not forget Johnny Appleseed. His real name was John Chapman. He traveled through the American frontier wilderness with a bag of apple seeds. That's probably why we have so many varieties. Apples were central and northern Europe's most important cultivated crop at the time of the discovery of America.

There are over 10,000 varieties and more on the way. Be daring, try a new variety! Because an apple tree does not grow true to seed, trees today are grafted. By grafting we take two or three varieties and hope we come up with another variety with the best attributes of both apples.

A good example of grafting is a fairly new apple called Jonagold. It's a cross between a Jonathan and a Golden Delicious. It is regarded as one of the best all-purpose apples — excellent for eating out of hand as well as for cooking. It stores well and is large, crisp, and juicy.

The Golden Delicious really gets a bum rap. It was a chance seedling found by Anderson H. Mullins. He sent three apples to Paul Stark of Stark Nursery, New York. The nursery had bought the Red Delicious, just 10 years before, so Paul named this new apple the Golden Delicious.

The Red and Golden Delicious are as different as night and day. The Red is a wonderful apple for eating. The Golden is good for everything from apple pie to salads.

When I was a child, we had a lot of the old varieties: Winesap, Gravenstein, Rome Beauty, Spitzenburg (my favorite), King, Jonathan, and Northern Spy. I am glad to say, here in the Willamette Valley, people have started to plant more of the old varieties. Now we have three new apple varieties that have been planted; all good apples: Gala, Braeburn, and Fuji.

The old saying, "an apple a day will keep the doctor away," should read, "an apple a day will keep the dentist away." Dentists praise the apple as a natural toothbrush. Doctors recommend them to teenagers as a complexion aid and to weight watchers because of their calorie count in relation to bulk. The pectin in apples is said to help maintain desired cholesterol levels. The combination of fruits high in pectin and cellulose content have long been know to help intestinal tone.

Learn to buy apples with your eyes and smell. Buy apples by the box in the fall; share with a friend or neighbor and you will save money. Store your treasure in a cool place; raise off of cement stacking the box on top of bricks or used tin cans.

For tasty baked apples in the microwave, try peeling a 1/2" strip all around the center of the apple. This will let it cook better! Core the apple, placing it in a micro-proof dish to catch the juice. Add brown sugar, raisins, and margarine in the center and bake on high four to six minutes. The power of microwave ovens vary so you may want to adjust the cooking time to your oven. Ymmmmmmm!

Due to weather conditions, there are times when salad greens are very high in cost. This is the time to make a waldorf salad — apples, celery, raisins, use yogurt or no-fat mayonnaise. The Waldorf Salad originated by a chef for the opening of the Waldorf-Astoria Hotel in New York City.

FRANK'S FACTS ON APPLES:

To choose a good apple, thump it easily with your fingers. It should have a crisp, sharp sound.

Dentists praise the apple as a natural toothbrush.

To keep apples from turning brown after slicing you must acidate the water using a pinch of salt, for every apple. If you can't use salt, try adding lemon juice or white wine to the water. This will keep the apples nice and white for a short time!

In a salad, Golden Delicious apples do not turn brown as fast as other apples. They are good keepers, too.

When baking a pie or making apple sauce, put the peel in your blender and add the juice to the top of your pie or sauce. You will have more apple flavor.

When baking an apple, if you prick the skins when raw, the skin will not split when baked in oven.

An apple ripens ten times faster at 50 degrees, and fifty times faster at 70 degrees. Keep your apples cool if you want a crisp apple — change your supply in the apple bowl on the table. Don't put out too many at a time.

A small apple contains about 58 calories.

In Persia, apples are considered the fruit of immortality. Apples are symbols of love and beauty in Greek and Roman Mythology.

The difference between apple cider and apple juice has always been a question. Both are products of fresh, undiluted juice of apples. Apple cider is fresh pressed apples, that's all. Apple juice is pasteurized and bottled for longer shelf life. It is filtered to remove all pulp.

Most apples are picked and put into cold storage in October.

PEARS

Fall is also the season for fresh pears. Over 80 percent of pears grown in the U.S. are from Washington, Oregon, and California. There are over 5,000 varieties known in Europe; here we are most familiar with the Bartlett, Anjou, Bosc, and Comice variety.

Don't throw away the wrappers when buying pears. Keep your pears wrapped in them, not only for protection but, to help the fruit ripen. You may also place green pears in a brown paper bag. Do not seal the bag — just squeeze it shut leaving a hole so a little gas can escape. Press gently around the stem end of the pear to test for ripeness, if it give to gentle pressure, the pear is ripe.

For a different treat, be sure to try an Asian pear. They are available from July to late October and are grown in California, Washington, Oregon, and Japan. This is the oldest cultivated pear known. The Asian pear is yellow skinned and you should buy them with your nose. A fragrant aroma is what you want and not a pear that yields to pressure. This pear is ripe when it is hard to the touch and is juicy and crisp when you bite it!

FRANK'S FACTS ABOUT PEARS

Pears, like apples, go into controlled atmosphere storage for longer shelf life.

It is best to use firm and slightly under-ripe pears for baking and cooking purposes.

Pears ripen from the inside out, so place them in a paper bag until they yield to gently pressure at the top of the stem end.

Remember, once a pear starts to ripen, there is no stopping it.

Pears have one ounce of fat and no sodium. They are high in fiber and potassium.

A chip on the shoulder is often a piece of wood that has fallen from the head!

Age is mostly a matter of mind, if you don't mind it doesn't matter.

PUMPKINS & SQUASH

October is also the month we celebrate Halloween. Large and small pumpkins are everywhere. The American custom of carving grotesque faces on pumpkins was a form of Thanksgiving celebration in older days.

The pumpkin was a symbol of the harvest and making a pumpkin into a jack-o'-lantern is reminiscent of the sun and the warmth which brought pumpkins out of the earth.

Pumpkins along with Indian corn and ornamental gourds are symbols of autumn. Keep the seeds of your pumpkin and roast them. An easy way to get the seeds away from the membrane is to put them all in a colander and turn on the water. The seeds will remain in the colander.

After you have separated the fiber from the seeds of a melon, pumpkin, squash, sunflower or watermelon, cover the seeds with salted water. Bring to a boil and simmer at least an hour and a half. Drain and dry on paper towels. Spread the seeds in a pie plate or shallow pan. Coat with vegetable oil and bake in a 350 degree oven until golden brown. From time to time, stir the seeds. You don't have to use salt if you don't want to. And you may choose to bake the seeds without the vegetable oil coating.

Pumpkins can be cooked like squash. Did you know that the pumpkin we buy for jack-o'-lantern carving is not the one used commercially for pie-making? In fact, most pumpkins pies are actually made from squash!

With fall starting, look for a large variety of winter squash. Make sure they are mature before you buy any large amount to store. Remember the thumb nail trick: a thumb nail that goes into the winter squash too easily tells me it is still green. Leave it on the vine a little longer.

When your winter squash is ready to harvest, make sure you put it in the hottest part of your house for 2 days. This removes the moisture. Then put it in a dry place. Rotate the stored squash once a month. If you have an old screen door in the garage, put the squash on the screen to keep the air circulating and to keep the squash off of cold spots. Remember, it takes rain and sunshine to make a rainbow!

FRANK'S FACTS ON SQUASH

Most pumpkin pies are actually made from squash. And pumpkins can be cooked like squash.

If a thumb nail goes easily into a winter squash, the squash is still too green. Leave it on the vine awhile longer.

Once you harvest squash, place it in the hottest part of the house for 2 days to remove the moisture. Then store the squash in a dry place. Rotate stored squash monthly.

POMEGRANATES

October is the month that 60 percent of the pomegranates are picked. The word pomegranate means apple with many seeds. How true it is.

Many years ago pomegranate trees or small shrubs were planted just as a wind-break between other crops in California. Today it is a big crop. There is a lot of demand for the fruit around the Christmas season where it has various meanings for many people.

In China the pomegranate is a fertility symbol. Women who desire children bring the fruit to the goddess of mercy. In her temple are pictures of pomegranates.

In order for a Turkish woman to find out how many children she will have, the bride will throw a pomegranate to the ground to break it. The number of seeds that come out of the shell is how many children she will bear. I'll bet if she threw it hard enough she could have a football team.

Grenadine for flavoring drinks comes from the juice. Don't cut through the fruit as the juice will stain everything it touches. Instead, break off the crown and SCORE all around the fruit with a knife. Hold the pomegranate in your hand and twist the fruit.

Pomegranate seeds freeze very well to use them later in vegetable or fruit salads, on ice cream, in tarts, blend for juice or just eat them like raisins. By Christmas the pomegranate season is over. If you need them, buy them ahead of time. They will keep well in the refrigerator crisper.

FRANK'S FACTS ON POMEGRANATES

Sixty percent of the pomegranate crop is picked in October.

Don't cut through the fruit because the juice will stain everything it touches.

Pomegranate means apple with many seeds.

The pomegranate season is over by the end of December, so buy early and refrigerate them if you want them for the holidays.

A man has two pennies; he should buy a loaf of bread with one which will sustain his life, and a flower with the other which will give him a reason to live.

Celebrations of harvest have been throughout history in various forms. It is a time when people who till the land take the time to give thanks for the harvest. The first Thanksgiving Day in the United States of America was celebrated at Plymouth Massachusetts.

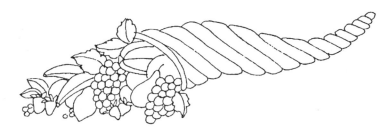

Thanksgiving and the eating of turkey is older than the Plymouth colony. It has been traced to the Mayans, who in 2000 B.C. dined on wild turkey. They set aside a day to play or watch a game in a stone-walled enclosure.

The Mayans would set two round hoops in the wall, about 12 feet high. Using a rock, they would try to put it through the hoop. I don't know if it is true or not, but when Betty and I were in Mexico, the guide told us that the winning team got to sacrifice the losing team. It is almost like our football games!

When you think about it you realize that times haven't changed much. Just the setting. We now sit in an enclosure, in front of a television set, eat turkey and watch football!

On October 3, 1864, President Abraham Lincoln set aside the last Thursday in November as Thanksgiving Day. Since then, many have referred to Thanksgiving

as "Turkey Day." Thanksgiving turkey without cranberries is like serving an undressed turkey — unthink-
able.

CRANBERRIES

Did you know that the cranberry, the sidekick of the
holiday turkey, is one of only three native American
fruits? Read on, and I will tell you what the other two
are.

For nearly 250 years, settlers harvested their cranberries from wild vines. Charles McFarlin built the first
cranberry bog in Oregon in 1885. Some of these bogs
are still producing after more than 100 years.

One theory of how the cranberry got its name is that
the blossom on its slender stem resembled the head
and neck of a crane. Cranberries are also called
bounce berries. Many years ago, cranberries were
sorted off a table where the bad fruit was picked off by
hand.

At that time, cranberries were stored in silos. One day,
as a farmer was taking a sack of berries down the
stairs, he dropped it. The cranberries bounced down
the stairs, but only the good berries made it all the
way to the landing. The bad berries remained on the
stairs. Today, a cranberry has to bounce seven times
over a wooden barrier before it can be packed!

The fresh cranberry season is short, so buy early.
Don't wait until Thanksgiving to buy your supply. It is

easy to freeze them. All you have to do is pop them in the freezer in the original package. If you change the packaging, be sure to put air holes in the bag. Buy more than one package to use throughout the year.

Betty and I were in Bandon, Oregon recently and were amazed at the amount of cranberries that are grown in our own back yard. Not too long ago a large percentage of the cranberry crop was sold fresh. Now I would be surprised if 50 percent goes to fresh market, with the rest being used in juice and other products.

Oh yes, the other two native American fruits are blueberries and concord grapes!

FRANK'S FACTS ON CRANBERRIES

The cranberry is one of three native American fruits.

The fresh cranberry season is short, so buy early. It is easy to freeze cranberries in their original package.

Cranberries are called bounce berries because the ripe berries bounce seven times over a barrier before they are packed.

A good wife and good health are a man's best wealth.

YAMS vs. SWEET POTATO

Let's settle the debate! The cartoon sailor character used to say, "I yam what I yam, and that's all that I yam." I'm glad to know he knew what a yam was. Everyone else tends to be confused. Today in parts of the United States, a yam is called a sweet potato and a sweet potato a yam.

Actually, the only true yam is a Name Yam (pronounced NAH-mee) that originated in Africa. It is a large tuber that is shaped like a log and looks like Big Foot's foot. It grows as big, too. In the South Pacific they have found some tubers that weigh over 500 lbs.

The Name Yam has a bland flavor to someone who has not grown up with it. It can be used the same way we use potatoes. Do not refrigerate a yam unless it is cooked. Keep in a dry place. They will not keep as long as potatoes.

What we know as yams and sweet potatoes are members of the Morning Glory family. The yam or sweet potato is not planted by seeds, but rather by starts or cuttings. It is placed in a hotbed to produce the cuttings and this is called the mother plant.

When father farmer is ready to plant, he breaks off the cuttings and plants them. Try planting a yam or sweet potato in your kitchen. Put it in a container with the stem end in four inches of water and watch it grow.

Yams have an orange color and are very moist. Sweet potatoes are white or ivory in color and are a bit drier than yams. Both rank high in nutritional value. Sliced yams are a wonderful addition to a vegetable tray as they taste great raw and also add color. Also consider making Sweet Potato fries. They are good!

So, what do sweet potatoes wear when they go to bed...they wear yammies!

FRANK'S FACTS ON YAMS AND SWEET POTATOES

The Name (NAH-mee) Yam is the only true yam and it's a large tuber shaped like a log.

Yams have an orange color and are very moist.

Do not refrigerate a yam unless it is cooked. Store in a dry place.

Yams can be used the same as white potatoes, but do not keep as long.

Yams and Sweet Potatoes are members of the Morning Glory family.

Sweet potatoes are white or ivory in color and are a bit drier than yams.

POTATOES

Did you know ounce for ounce a potato has the same number of calories as an apple. That's right. It has fewer calories than a cup of yogurt, or a 3 oz. hamburger pattie, or a 1/2 cup of cottage cheese. The only problem we have with the potato is it tastes so good with sour cream and butter.

Most of us need more of the natural fiber, vitamins, and minerals that the potato provides. This may come as a surprise, but potatoes provide 20% of the vitamin C in the U.S. food supply. Potatoes contain no fat.

To keep potatoes for any length of time, put them in a cool, dry place. A lot of people put them under the sink, next to the dishwasher, or next to the dry onions. It isn't long before your onions sprout, as the potato gives off a gas that causes the onions to sprout.

A dark place is best, as the light is what turns potatoes green. If the skin becomes green, peel away any green before using.

New potatoes and old potatoes confuse some people. A new potato is one that the skins are not yet set. When the vines are killed, usually by a frost, the skins are set and are what we call the old potato. They are put in a potato cellar and packaged as they are needed.

I go back to before they had a lot of potato cellars. In fact, I remember buying 200 sacks of potatoes at

$1.00 per sack. That's 1 cent per pound. I guess that surely dates me. For the sake of the farmers, I am glad they built more potato cellars.

When planting a potato crop, "hill-up" the dirt by creating a mound of dirt. Then when you want to harvest those special little potatoes, run your fingers through the dirt and take what you want. Then, "hill-up" the dirt again and the potatoes in the ground will keep on growing. In Oregon, we don't have the ground freeze like some states, so you can leave the potatoes in the ground year around. Even states with cold ground freeze can keep them in ground, if covered with more dirt or leaves. In any case, just don't let them have air or light.

Many years ago vegetables were called garden sauce or just sass to go with meat. Potatoes and onion were called short sauce. Carrots and beets were called long sauce. I guess I was called a sauce man who was a person who sold vegetables from door to door.

You should learn to buy potatoes with your eyes. A ten pound bag of potatoes cost between $1.00 and $2.00. Baking potatoes cost between $3.90 to $4.90 for 10 pounds. The baking potatoes are marked as bakers while the 10 pound bag isn't marked, but they bake every bit as well as the higher priced ones.

> When opportunity knocks, some people are in the backyard looking for four-leaf clovers.

FRANK'S FACTS ON POTATOES

There are over 5,000 different ways to cook potatoes!

Store potatoes in a dry, dark place. Rotate your potatoes every time you take some out of your container. Potatoes touching one another will cause moisture if you don't.

Remember, keep your potatoes away from the dry onions because they give off gases that cause onions to grow and sprout.

After cutting onions, and you want to eliminate the onion smell from the knife, just run the knife through a potato.

Too much salt in your soup? Just drop a peeled potato in the soup and it will absorb the salt.

Keep the water that you boiled potatoes to use in soup and stews. Instead of using cold milk to add to your mashed potatoes, use the hot potato water with powdered milk for healthy, HOT mashed potatoes.

A round slice of raw potato will draw the heat out of your eyes.

> There is no traffic jam on the extra mile!

PERSIMMONS

November is a good month to enjoy persimmons, a soft textured winter fruit with a shiny brilliant orange skin and red and orange meat. It is sometimes called the "Apple of the Orient." There are over 500 varieties of persimmons, each with a different color, texture and shape.

It is the acorn shaped Hachiya that makes up over 90 percent of our planting. A hachiya must be very soft to enjoy. A firm one will cause your mouth to pucker because of the tannin it contains. The high tannic acid disappears when the fruit is completely ripe or even better when overripe.

Hachiyas freeze very well and that is the best way to preserve them. They will last three months to one year. You just cut off the pointed tip, wrap tightly, them pop them in your freezer, but let them ripen so that they are soft to the touch before freezing. When you want to use it the fruit will be ready to eat after thawing at room temperature. But then the fruit must be used right away.

The Hachiyas can be ripened by wrapping in foil and placing in the freezer, but it will lose some flavor.

A newer variety of persimmon had come into the market called Fu Yu. It has a flatter shape. This persimmon has no tannin, so it should be eaten hard and crisp like an apple.

The Fu Yu does not freeze well, but it is excellent to eat fresh and is a delicious piece of fruit to add to your salad.

The wood of the persimmon tree is from the ebony family and is used to make golf clubs. The leaves fall from the tree, leaving fruit on the branches. The tree looks as if it has been decorated for Christmas. In California, I have enjoyed this view early in the autumn mornings when the dew gives the tree a very special look.

FRANK'S FACTS ABOUT PERSIMMONS

There are over 500 varieties of persimmons, each with a different texture, color, and shape.

The Hachiya is the most popular with 90 percent of our planting. It must be very soft to enjoy.

The Hachiyas may be ripened by wrapping in foil and placing in the freezer, but it will lose some flavor.

A new variety of persimmon is the Fu Yu which should be eaten hard like an apple and is excellent in salad.

> The greatest reward for serving others is the satisfaction found in your own heart.

This Thanksgiving Day let's give thanks for what we have and share our bounty with others who may be alone for the holiday. Help serve dinner at a homeless shelter. Pick up a few extra groceries the next time you are out shopping and drop them off at a food bank.

Sharing with someone less fortunate can help them through a rough time and as an added bonus make you feel good inside. Happy Thanksgiving!

Every child has a right to be both well-fed and well-led.

Only in a world of love can we unfold and bloom.

DECEMBER

With the holidays approaching we can look forward to an abundance of sweet Washington navel oranges, seedless Satsuma mandarins, crisp Red and Golden Delicious apples among other treats to fill our holiday baskets.

December is a good time to stock up on box fruit. Especially if you intend to give fruit baskets as holiday gifts! Or, split a box with a neighbor or friend and you can save some money. Keep some of the apples or oranges in the refrigerator, the fruit will keep longer.

The holidays are a time of family traditions. Caroling, the yule log, stockings hung by the fireplace or pot-bellied stove, decorating the tree, and midnight candlelight church services are just a few in my memory.

As a child, on Christmas Eve, we would hang our stockings by the pot-bellied stove. In the morning, we would have a Satsuma, an orange, and a walnut or chestnut in the toe! It is a tradition I have passed on to my own children. We also put out cookies and milk for Santa. Is that why Santa is so plump? Maybe we should have given him a traditional gift of fruit instead. And don't forget to give the reindeer a carrot so they can see in the dark!

Traditions are a great way to keep in touch with the past. Ask your parents or grandparents about traditions that they remember and start some of your own. Our family has a wreath made of pine cones that we gathered on a road trip to Yellowstone National Park many years ago. Every time we hang it over the fireplace, it brings back good memories.

In America, Christmas isn't Christmas without colorful stockings hanging on the mantel. There will be one for each member of the family. Legend says that St. Nicholas threw gold coins down the chimney which fell into the stockings drying at the hearth. Gold coins have since been replaced with oranges, tangerines, cookies, toys, and trinkets.

ORANGES

The Washington Navel is the finest eating orange. (No I haven't lost my marbles). It is seedless, with orange skin and sweet flesh divided into nine to eleven segments.

In 1870, through assistance of a missionary stationed in Brazil, twelve navel orange trees were sent in tubs to Washington, D.C., hence the name. Mr. and Mrs. Luther Tibbets took two of the trees to Riverside, California. These two trees started the extensive plantings that we see in California today.

It is now generally recognized that one of the outstanding events in the economic and social development of California was the introduction of the orange in 1873. So the Washington Navel orange doesn't come from our northern neighbor, but our southern one!

In buying oranges, don't let the green color fool you. When the fruit is fully ripe, and it hangs on the tree during the warm weather, it begins to turn green from the stem end. It is called re-greening. The warm ground temperature returns the chlorophyll to the skins.

TANGERINES & MANDARINS

There are many varieties of tangerines and mandarins. Each one has a season. The Dancy variety has a sweet-tart flavor with many seeds. It is loose and easy to peel. It was named for Colonel G. L. Dancy. He called it a tangerine with a kid-glove skin.

The Minneola Tangelo is a cross between a tangerine and a pomelo. The flavor is good with a grapefruit-like tartness. A tangelo is a cross between a TANGerine (the first four letters) and a pomELO (the last three letters).

The Murcott is named honey tangerine. It is very sweet, with a thin rind that is easy to peel. It is full of juice.

The Temple orange took over ten years to get its name changed to Royal Mandarin. It is juicy, but has lots of seeds. It makes wonderful juice. The name change has helped the fruit sell better. It is believed to be a cross between a tangerine and an orange.

To most people in the U.S., the name tangerine applies to all zipper skin citrus marketed. However, tangerine is the name for only one type of mandarin.

For a special treat, try some of the zipper skinned mandarins. Many people make the mistake of looking for tangerines and mandarins without knowing which variety they like. If you want a seedless, sweet mandarin, ask for a Satsuma. It is my favorite and is easy to peel. November and December are the months you can find a good supply of Satusmas.

At one time all Satsumas came from Japan in little wooden boxes, but today a large share of the market is grown in California.

FRANK'S FACTS ON MANDARINS & TANGERINES

Tangerine is the name for only one type of mandarin.

If you want a seedless, sweet mandarin ask for a Satsuma. It is easy to peel.

A tangelo is a cross between a tangerine (first four letters) and a pomelo (the last three letters). The flavor is a grapefruit-like tartness.

November and December are the months to find good supplies of Satsumas.

CHESTNUTS

The crisp days and nights make me want to roast chestnuts by the open fire, actually I use the microwave, but the results are the same. Many of us remember the poem "...under the spreading chestnut tree..." but it must have been written before the turn of the century since most of the chestnut trees in the U.S. were killed by a blight. Today, the chestnut tree is making a comeback with new disease-resistant varieties.

It is so easy to roast chestnuts in your microwave. Cut an "x" on one side, rinse them leaving only the water that remains on the nut and put them in a microwave safe dish. Cook at 1/2 power for 4.5 to 5.5 minutes (adjusting time and power for your microwave), peel and enjoy. Many people enjoy them roasted the original way (in the fire) or boiled for about 30 minutes, again after they have been scored with "x."

AVOCADO

Some people use avocado on both their fruit and vegetable trays. Avocados have been around for a long time, as early as 291 B.C. In fact, at one time they were called the alligator pear. The Calavo people have done such a good job of promoting the avocado that a lot of people ask for Calavos when that is just a brand name.

It is best to buy avocados when they are green and ripen them at home. Don't use your fingers to test them to see if they are ripe. If you do, you will cause black marks to appear on the fruit, Instead, cup the avocado gently in your hand; a little pressure will tell you it is ripe. they are very easy to ripen. Put them in a brown paper bag with an apple or banana peel. Do not seal the bag, just squeeze it shut.

When I am teaching a produce class, the audience is always amazed at my method of removing the avocado pit! Of course, we begin by slicing the avocado in half from end to end. Gently twist the halves to separate. In my class, I always spoon out the delicious, green fruit and I suggest that the avocado shell may be used as a serving container for your guacamole dip!

I hold up the half with the pit in my hand, and with the knife in the other hand, I gently strike the pit with the knife and cleanly lift the pit from the avocado. The pit is stuck to the knife blade. Then I begin to discuss what to do with the pit, after the audience has finished exclaiming and chuckling!

What can be done with the avocado pit, besides planting an avocado? Try putting the pit in with your avocado dip; it will help keep the dip from turning brown. If you are using half of your avocado, put some lemon juice on the other half and replace the pit in the avocado half and it will also help keep it from turning brown.

FRANK'S FACTS ON AVOCADOS

Lift the avocado pit easily from the fruit meat by gently striking it with a sharp knife. It will amaze you by how this simply works.

It is best to buy avocados when they are green and ripen them at home.

Ripen them quickly either in a brown paper bag with an apple or banana peel but don't seal the sack. Or, wrap the avocado in tin foil to enhance the ripening. Do not put unripe avocados in the refrigerator.

Avocados may be used on fruit or vegetable trays.

FRANK'S FACTS ON HOLIDAY TRAYS

For your holiday gathering, spice up your relish dishes with something different than the usual carrots, celery, and cucumbers. To add some color, try raw yam sticks, jicama slices, or one of my favorites daikon.

Daikon is a white radish that can grow as long as three feet. That's a long radish! The Chinese pickle daikon in brine the same way that Americans pickle cucumbers. The pickled daikon radish adds flavor and zest to their diet. To sweeten the flavor of yams and daikon, put the sliced vegetable in a saltwater bath and then rinse in clear water.

Liven up your fruit platters with papaya or kiwi along with oranges, tangerines and apples. Grapes or pomegranate seeds sprinkled on top makes a beautiful display. Of course, you may include avocados on either your fruit or vegetable trays.

HOLIDAY BASKETS

As I demonstrated during a recent produce class, preparing holiday baskets for gift giving is as simple as smiling. Of course, the container for the goodies may be many things. I choose the traditional wicker baskets of any size or a lovely, decorative glass bowl as a suggestion. And then I get creative with container ideas. How about a colorful, plastic colander? Or a pottery bowl? Or a metal bucket? Or one of many ideas you may have!

To save money on this gift idea, buy your fruit by the box. Apples, pears, tangerines, kiwi, pomegranate, grapefruit, oranges, avocados, pineapple...

The important basis for holiday basket building is to start with a good base. Oranges, or any solid fruit will do. Then begin building your basket adding a little bit of everything, or use only what you know your friends like. Add some of your own special, homemade goodies.

I save the papers from the wrapped pears for a few reasons. One of them is to stick a few in and about the fruit for a more festive look! The other reason will be discussed in the tomato facts, in the Produce for All Seasons chapter. And you'll need to save your pear box, too!

I love to use a delicious pineapple for the center of any holiday basket. The pineapple is a sign of hospitality, in addition to tasting wonderful. A holiday basket like this is a gift from the heart, and it is healthy for the heart, too!

HOLIDAY GIVING IDEAS

Now is the time to ship fruit to all your friends and relatives. Don't wait until it's too late. The receiver will enjoy it a few days early.

There are new varieties of fruits and vegetables on the market these days. Be adventuresome and try them. One of my favorites is the small Lady apple. The Lady apple is about the size of an apricot, has a red and golden color and is sweet tasting. Children like them because they can fit in a pocket for a quick snack. The Lady apple and Seckel pear are used in the traditional delarobia wreath.

If you are mailing home baked goods or preserves, be sure to enclose the ingredient list. Many people are allergic or may have a medical condition to consider.

This Christmas and Holiday Season, let's give peace on earth a chance. A note of thanks to anyone sending a gift, large or small, is a good way to start. Do it while you think about it. Like me, sometimes I say I'll do it later, but later never seems to come. Try to make Christmas a year-long experience and may God bless your home.

APPLES

No produce book would be complete without a segment on apples; the varieties and what you can do with some, but not with others. Todays apples are quite a bit more expensive than when I was growing up. In fact, when my brother Lawrence leased the produce section at 36th & Hawthorne from Fred Meyers, he bought a home orchard of apples for $100.00. This was in 1938. We picked eight hundred boxes of apples from that orchard. We sold them at 49 cents for a forty pound box. Today, only during October and November can you buy one pound for that price. Allow me to introduce you to some apples in alphabetical order:

AKANE, or Prime Red apples are fairly new to the Northwest. It was introduced by Japan in 1970. It is a bright red apple and all purpose for pies, sauces, salads, eating out of hand, and baking.

BALDWIN apple originated in Wilmington, Massachusetts around 1740. It is not very popular anymore because it takes around ten years to bear fruit. It is a good all purpose apple.

BRAEBURN apple is another new-comer to the Northwest. It is a fine apple for eating. Its color is red with green highlights. The Braeburn is crispy and sweet-tart which is good for snacks and salads. It is one of the apples of the nineties.

The CORTLAND apple is a cross between a Ben Davis and a McIntosh. It entered the market around

1915. It is crisp, juicy, and sweetly tart. It is in great demand because its white flesh resists browning and it is a good all-purpose apple.

CRITERION apples is a cross between a Red Delicious and a Golden Delicious. It is very crisp and juicy and has the best flavors of both apples. This is a wonderful eating apple.

ELSTAR apple is a new variety obtained by crossing Golden Delicious with other varieties. The flesh has a crunchy taste and is very juicy. It is large, golden yellow and has a red bloom. The Elstar has a wonderful aroma. You'll find them in the market between October and December. It is best for eating out of hand, snacks, and baking.

FUJI apple is another new apple to the Northwest. It is mild-sweet-snappy crisp. It is excellent for eating out of hand. Growers are planting more Fuji apple trees. The Fuji is a winner this time for apple lovers.

The GALA apple is a hybrid from New Zealand. It is a sweet apple with excellent texture and flavor. This apple, along with the Braeburn and Fuji will be the three new apples of the nineties. The Gala is an all-purpose apple.

GOLDEN DELICIOUS apple was discovered in West Virginia in 1914, when it was called Mullins Yellow Seedling. It is rated as the second best seller at this time. It was bought by the Stark Brothers Nursery of New York and was renamed Yellow or Golden Delicious. This is a good all-purpose apple.

The GRANNY SMITH apple originated about 1865 in Australia. It is a very tart, green apple. This is a good keeper and has a high acid flavor. It is a good all-purpose apple.

GRAVENSTEIN apples are one of the best for applesauce. They make wonderful, full flavor pies. Gravenstein is also good for snacks, salads, and baking.

IDARED apples developed in 1942 as a cross between a Jonathan and a Wagener apple. It is an all-purpose apple especially good for snacks and desserts. It is wonderful for baking.

The JONAGOLD apple is a cross between a Jonathan and a Golden Delicious. It is a superior apple for eating, and good for applesauce and pies. It has the perfect balance of tartness and sweetness.

JONATHAN apple was called the Rick Apple in 1820. It was discovered in Woodstock, New York. Because it holds its shape so well, it is in demand for baking whole and in pies.

The LADY is a small apple originated in France during medieval times. It is used for Christmas decorations and it is delicious to eat fresh. It is small enough to fit in a purse or pocket for that extra snack.

LODI is a very early apple, and is not a good keeper. It is fine for cooking purposes and makes wonderful sauce.

The McINTOSH apple was discovered by John McIntosh in Ontario, Canada in 1830. It is excellent to eat fresh in the autumn. It is good for snacks, salad, pies, sauce, and is a good dessert apple.

The MELROSE apple became the official Ohio State Apple in 1970. It is a cross between Red Delicious and Jonathan. It is crispy, juicy, and a good all-purpose apple.

NEWTOWN PIPPIN apple was discovered in Newtown, Long Island, New York in 1700. It is one of the oldest and best varieties to be found in commercial production. It is firm, crisp, juicy, and the sweetly tart flesh makes it ideal for pie-filling and sauce.

NORTHERN SPY is one of my favorites. It originated in East Bloomfield, New York around 1800. It does not bear every year. It is a good all-purpose apple and freezes well.

The RED DELICIOUS apple was originally called Hawkeye when it was discovered in 1872 in Peru, Iowa. The name was changed by the Stark Brothers of New York, to Delicious in 1895. It is best used for salads, fruit cups, and eating out of hand.

The ROME BEAUTY was found growing in Rome, Ohio in 1816. That's how it got its name. Rome

Beauties are good for baking as they hold their shape and flavor.

SPARTON apples are a cross between Yellow Newtown and McIntosh. It has white flesh, crisp and juicy. It stores very well and is a good all-purpose apple.

SPITZENBERG apples were a favorite of both Presidents Washington and Jefferson, and Frank Comella, too! The Spitzenberg originated in New York in 1770. The flavor of the Spitz is rich and aromatic, an apple I remember from my youth. It is a very good keeper, although it doesn't produce every year. It is a good all-purpose apple.

WINTER BANANA apple is a 100 year old variety. It originated in Indiana. It has pink on yellow cheeks and a flavor of bananas.

One October, when I was in Hood River, Oregon, a grower was cutting out his winter banana apple trees. He cut them leaving two feet of tree standing. He split the top and planted the Gala root stock in the split. Using the winter banana rooting system, next year he will have Galas instead of Winter Bananas. Sadly, this is happening to a lot of old time apples.

The apple is the most important fruit species in the northern hemisphere. It has more varieties than any other fruit species.

> The best antique is an old friend.

BANANAS

Would you believe me if I told you bananas are berries and what they grow on isn't a tree, but just a huge tropical plant? Both are true. Actually, a banana plant is a herb. The stalk is made of fiber rather than wood. Another little known fact is that bananas are pound for pound the most widely sold fruit in the U.S.

The banana made its first official debut in 1876 at the Centennial Exhibition in Philadelphia, Pennsylvania. Wrapped in foil, they sold for 10 cents each. The bananas we eat today are imported from Central America. What was once a luxury can now be enjoyed every day.

The typical banana has about 88 calories and only .2 grams of fat, hardly a trace of sodium and is high in fiber and potassium. In fact, it is the first fruit usually introduced to a new baby's diet!

The first time I saw a banana growing was on a trip to Mexico. Betty and I had to take a cab to the resort. We passed a banana grove, and I got so excited seeing them that I told to driver to stop. He must have thought, "What a crazy Italian, just to get excited over what I see every day." It was a wonderful feeling for me to see the groves and to take pictures. You would have thought I'd won the lottery.

RED BANANAS have a bit sweeter flavor than a yellow banana. This short, squat banana has a peel that is purple red when ripe and the flesh is creamy white with a tinge of light pink.

MANZANO BANANAS look like a short, stubby banana. It has a banana flavor that is accented by that of strawberries and apples.

NITAS or SMALL BABY BANANAS are a smaller version of mature bananas. Nitas are a good serving size and are popular with the airline industry because it fits nicely on the food plates. You can try having carmel or chocolate bananas using Nitas; or try frying them.

All bananas are gassed by Ethylene gas which is the same gas that is put into fruit to ripen by mother nature.

When you buy bananas — number one, don't pull one at a time selecting from various bunches (we call them by body parts, namely hands and fingers!). If you select your banana supply by the finger, your bananas will not keep very long. Number two, select four or five fingers from a green hand, and four or five fingers from a ripened hand of bananas. By the time the ripe ones are gone, the green fingers will be ripe!

A banana will keep up to 5 days in the refrigerator (yes, I said refrigerator), but be sure and put them in at the stage you enjoy them. They will not ripen any more. The skin will turn black, but the banana is still edible. If you want to freeze ripe bananas, leave them in their skin, or peel and wrap each banana in plastic.

Then you can mash your bananas before freezing to be added to your banana bread when thawed. Or, you can put a peeled frozen banana, with ice cream or frozen yogurt, plus a little milk in your blender and have a delicious banana milkshake.

Try peeling the banana from the blossom end, instead of the stem end. That's the way the monkeys do it. For one thing, you won't bruise it and you will also have a handle on your banana. Children will find peeling a banana easier this way.

Every so often when I go on a binge, I have a big banana split with the works. Yummy! Enjoy banana milkshakes, banana creme pie, banana bread, but most of all enjoy!

FRANK'S FACTS ON BANANAS

Bananas are the number one fruit in America. Over 25 pounds of bananas are consumed per person per year.

There is no such thing as a banana tree.

A big banana has only 95 calories. They have almost no fat or sodium. Bananas are a wonderful source of potassium and other vitamins.

Athletes consume more bananas than even the most avid, healthy eaters.

Bananas are available all year round and they are harvested every day of the year.

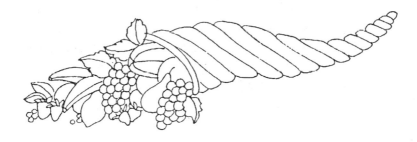

Don't make love by the garden gate.
Love is blind, but the neighbors ain't.

CELERY

Celery was first grown in Kalamazoo, Michigan in 1805. When the trains stopped there, growers would board them and go down the aisle saying, "Buy my celery." It must have been a wonderful thing for the passengers to see fresh vegetables. As you know, raw celery is part of our life. What would Thanksgiving be without a tray of celery? You need it as a stir stick in a Bloody Mary. It makes a perfect snack for dieters.

Celery was used as medicine by the Chinese in 1640. As late as 1722, celery was still referred to as a herb eaten to purify the blood. Celery leaves can be dried and used as a herb. Check your microwave book on how to do it.

Before 1950, celery had to be blanched by keeping the sun light off of the growing plant. It was accomplished by putting shingles up the side of the green celery, or piling dirt up the side. In 1950 and 1953, the Utah variety that we have today was developed. It is referred to as Pascal Celery. It stays green, but is nice and sweet, and it doesn't need blanching.

Try celery sticks with peanut butter. The small leaves are wonderful in tuna salad. For a special treat, try a Waldorf Salad, using apples, celery and mayonnaise, walnuts, and raisins.

Having trouble sleeping at night? Try counting celery seeds in a pound of seeds. There are over one million seeds to a pound. Don't you just hate it when you have limp celery? You buy nice, crisp celery and after a week it is not crisp anymore. That's because you take off one rib at a time to use. Then you put the rest back in the refrigerator. Well, those days are over.

First, remove the rubber band from your celery. The band will choke it. Trim the celery leaves and put them away for soup or dry them for later use. You must never cut off the butt end of the celery stalk and instead of pulling at ribs, just cut as much as needed from the top of the stalk.

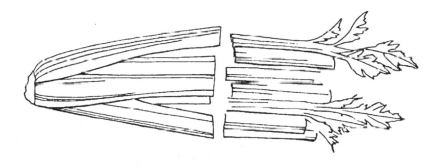

If you need a cup of fresh celery, slice about 4 inches from the top of the stalk. Second, take the stalk over to the sink, dip it in water, shake off excess water, put it in a plastic bag and refrigerate in the vegetable crisper. You have just put the moisture back in your celery.

The next time you cut celery, take the rest of the celery stalk and dip in water. Again, shake out the excess water and return it to the refrigerator. Celery will keep up to a month by using this method. Not only that, but you get part of your refrigerator back to put in your bananas!

Celery comes into the store all the same length. I wondered how it was done. When I was in California, I was taken through a celery packing plant. The celery went in the water, then to a moving belt. Employees put the celery all one direction. Half way down the belt there is a saw just like they have in the lumber industry. The saw cuts the leaves off to the right size. Now I know why they put the celery all the same direction.

FRANK'S FACTS ON CELERY

Celery leaves can be dried and used as a herb.

Remove the band from your celery when you get home, dip celery in water to moisturize. Shake away excess water and put in a plastic bag to refrigerate.

Never cut the butt end of celery from your stalk.

Remember to put the moisture back into your celery after each use.

CELERIAC or CELERY ROOT

Celeriac is also called Celery Root. It has a thick tuberous base and root which is the edible part. It may be served raw or cooked. The skin is tough and stringy. Keep celery root in your refrigerator crisper.

Raw celeriac can be peeled and cut in strips. Marinate the strips in french dressing for an hour. Then drain, squeezing slightly to remove excess liquid. Mix with mayonnaise and serve well chilled on crisp lettuce leaves.

Peeled and diced celery root may be cooked in boiling, salted water and will be tender in 10 minutes. A little vinegar and lemon juice added to the water will keep the celeriac white.

In Europe, the celery root is a vegetable that makes up part of their menu.

Did you hear about the guy who ate nothing but dehydrated food? It worked great until he drank a glass of water and gained 40 pounds!

COCONUTS

Coconuts are one of the ten most useful trees known to mankind. It has been said that it is one tree that can give a person all things that are necessary to sustain life. Now that is a big order.

A coconut tree lives to be 50 to 100 years. It has over 80 coconuts per year. The tree reaches a height of 50 feet and is able to withstand storms, heavy rains, or prolonged drought.

All parts of the coconut palm can be used. The fibers are made into huts, hats, mats, rope, upholstery, and boat caulking. The thick part of the leaves become oars. The tree trunk is used to make canoes. The hard coconut shell is used to make bowls and eating utensils. The shell is also used as fuel and makes fine charcoal.

When a coconut is very young, the flesh is soft and is used as a dessert. Many people think that when they break a coconut and the liquid comes out that it is coconut milk. This is not true. It is the water of the coconut. Coconut milk, which people use for cooking, is the white coconut that they twist with cheese cloth or fibers and remove. The white coconut meat is eaten. How about a big beautiful coconut creme pie?

When the meat is dried in the shell it is called Copra. The dry copra is ground into a pale yellow oil which is very important to making soap, cosmetics, and even shaving cream. Commercial sugar is made from sap taken from the unopened flower buds. And how about the roots? They are chewed by the natives for its narcotic affect.

When Betty and I won a trip to Playa Blanca, Mexico, we really found out how wonderful a coconut can be. One of the high officials took four of us to his home. It was a big villa. When we arrived he said we were probably thirsty. He called a worker over and before we knew it, up, up, up the tree he went. He threw down six or so large coconuts and it amazed me how he went up and down the tree so fast.

Then he took them into the villa and soon return with a work of art — flowers, fruit, and this coconut with a little umbrella and straw in it which we all enjoyed. All I can say is I was glad our host was driving because it was also filled with rum and other liquid. I don't think we will ever forget the coconut and the hospitality that was extended.

There are many ways to crack a coconut. You can freeze it or put it in an oven for 30 minutes at 350 degrees F. The easiest method is to drain the liquid by piercing the soft spots. Then tap around the coconut with a hammer until the hard shell falls off.

My cousin went on a diet for three months, eating bananas and coconuts. No, he didn't lose any weight, but you ought to see him climb trees! Just kidding!

LEMONS & LIMES

LEMONS are our most underrated fruit. They are available year long. Lemons have blossoms and mature fruit on the tree at the same time. California and Arizona produce virtually all the lemons grown in North America. Florida led the United States in lemon production until late in the 19th century. Heavy freeze in 1835 and again in 1894 ruined the crop and Floridians did not replant until recent years.

The 1849 California Gold Rush was the big start of lemon groves in that state. An outbreak of scurvy hit the population due to their living conditions and lack of vitamin C in their diet.

When it was discovered that vitamin C cured scurvy, a new industry of lemon-growers was born by 1856. Lemon originally meant sour tree.

Lemons added to vegetables like cauliflower, mushroom, artichoke will help keep them from turning color. Lemon may be used in a salad instead of oil dressings for those dieting. Grind lemon in your garbage disposal to keep it smelling fragrantly fresh!

To keep lemons for months, put them in a jar of water with the lid on and place in the refrigerator. You can get more juice out of a lemon by putting them in the microwave at full power for 30 seconds. Rolling it on the countertop helps the lemon get soft also.

To get a small amount of juice from a fresh lemon without shortening the life of the lemon, prick it with the tines of a fork and squeeze the needed amount of juice. Use lemon for flavoring fruits and vegetables.

Fresh lemon is also a beauty aid. Rub a lemon against your face to cleanse and close pores.

When your lemon supply needs to be used, remove the ice cubes from your freezer trays and fill the trays with the squeezed lemon juice. After frozen, put the lemon cubes in a plastic bag and you may use them later for ice tea or lemonade.

LIMES can be stored in the same sealed jar of water with your lemons. Won't that be a beautiful sight each time you open your refrigerator door? When Betty and I were in Mexico, a bartender showed me how he kept his limes in a box with sand over them. He kept them for weeks this way.

Tahiti (Persian) limes are a large fruit, while the Mexican limes are smaller with very thin rinds and greenish yellow color at maturity.

Persian limes should have a glossy, green skin and be heavy for their size. Limes are divided into acid and sweet types, however, only the acid limes are grown commerically in the U.S.

Do you know why the British sailors were called-limeys? They used limes daily as a cure for scurvy. A bite of lime with their spot of tea would give them the needed vitamin C to eliminate scurvy. In Livermore, England, the warehouse to keep limes was called a limehouse. And the warehouse was located on Lime Street.

FRANK'S FACTS ON LEMONS & LIMES

Lemon originally meant sour tree. Lemons have blossoms and mature fruit on a tree at the same time.

Rolling a lemon on the countertop helps the lemon become juicier.

Lemons added to cauliflower, mushroom, or artichoke will help keep them from turning color.

Lemon may be used on salads instead of oil dressings.

To keep lemons and limes for months, put them in a jar of water with a lid and place in the refrigerator.

Both lemons and limes may have their juice squeezed and frozen in ice cube trays. Then bag the cubes in plastic for later use.

If fate hands you a lemon, try making lemonade.

LETTUCE & SPINACH

We have five different kinds of lettuce and there is as many varieties of each kind. We have Iceberg, Romaine, Bibb or Boston, Looseleaf or Bunching, and Stem lettuce. With these we can get a lot of "sal." Sal is the Latin word for salad because salt was the only dressing used on greens. My how times have changed!

ICEBERG LETTUCE

Iceberg lettuce is shipped from California or Arizona. These states grow 90 percent of our crop. Years ago this lettuce was named Iceberg because when I was growing up, lettuce was packed as a layer of ice, layer of lettuce, another layer of ice, another layer of lettuce until three dozen heads of lettuce was packed. It was heavy and wet. The industry has come a long way since then. Today, in order to get it to us, lettuce is run through a vacuum cooler. It draws out all the heat.

Iceberg is the head lettuce we see in the store. It should be crisp and green. Good, fresh lettuce will keep and be crisp when you use it. When you buy it, take it home, cut out the core and put the moisture back into your lettuce. I know you have been told to hit it on the sink and pull out the core.

Today, we have stainless steel knives that you can use to core it. It doesn't bruise this way and please make sure you cut out all of the core. There is usually a runner off to one side. Now take it over to the faucet and run water where you took out the core. Put it on the dish strainer and let it drip dry. Take a small paper towel, put it over the end to catch any moisture, then put it in the plastic bag to refrigerate.

ROMAINE LETTUCE

Romaine lettuce has a long, loaf shaped head with long narrow leaves. The leaves appear coarse, but are very sweet and tender. The leafy lettuce also needs moisture put back in. Don't cut off the butt end of Romaine. Dip the head in water and shake out the excess water. Place it in a plastic bag (remember the easy way!) and refrigerate. Each time you use your lettuce, remember to check the moisture. You will know when you have to dip it again.

BIBB OR BOSTON LETTUCE

Bibb or Boston lettuce has a compact, globular head and are distinguished by their soft pliable leaves and delicate buttery flavor. The leaves form the head by overlapping one another in a smooth, regular manner. Try this lettuce with a vinegar dressing. That reminds me of a story...

On one of my trips down to California to buy produce, I told the cab driver to take me to a nice restaurant that had good food. When he stopped in front of a small restaurant, he told me this was what I was look- ing for so I went in and ordered my dinner. After eating my bibb lettuce and vinaigrette dressing salad, I knew he was right! Of course, I discovered later that the cab driver had a cousin working there. Wonderful food, wonderful memories.

Bibb or Boston lettuce are two varieties of Butterhead lettuce. Limestone was from Bibb lettuce seed, only it was grown in limestone. I understand they have their own seed now. All are excellent in salads. Again, dip and moisturize this lettuce but don't soak it.

LOOSELEAF OR BUNCHING LETTUCE

Green Leaf and Red Leaf are types of this lettuce. This type does not form heads. Green leaf is used to dress up vegetable trays because of its long shelf life. Red leaf is very tender, beautiful in color and wonderful in mixed green salads. Make sure you buy fresh red or leaf lettuce. Do not cut off the butt end of the lettuce.

Whon you gct it home, dip it in walei, shake out all excess water and put in a plastic bag and refrigerate in the crisper. Every so often when you use it, dip it again. You'll be keeping in the moisture, but don't soak it.

STEM LETTUCE

Celtuce, or Stem Lettuce, originated in Tibet, China. Celtuce is the only variety where you eat the stem and not the leaves. It has leaves similar to Romaine type lettuce. The edible stem has a flavor between a summer squash and an artichoke. The stem is very tasty and may be cooked like broccoli. When the Celtuce leaves are very young they are used in salad, but as the leaves get older they become hard and bitter.

MESCLUM GREENS

The name Mesclum is given to a mixture of small salad greens. The greens are picked by cutting a few leaves at a time, namely Red Oak, Frisee, Red Radicchio, Parsley, sprigs of Cherivl, and other small greens which are used in the mixture. Mixtures like this are called saladist — or cut-and-come-up-again crop. It is an expensive mixture, but a little goes a long way. Put in a plastic bag but don't force it in. Leave it loose in the bag. Store in the vegetable crisper in the refrigerator, but use as soon as possible.

RADICCHIO

Radicchio is a round, crisp, purple and white lettuce with an interesting bittersweet taste that is excellent mixed with Romaine or Boston lettuce. It is shipped from Italy and we are now starting to grow it in the U.S. It is shaped like a cabbage rose and has shiny, smooth leaves with white central ribs.

Radicchio is the Italian name for chicory. Slice the leaves as you need them, not before hand. Radicchio will keep in a plastic bag, but be sure to pack it loosely.

When it is stewed in white wine, garlic, and fresh basil, it turns into a rusty brown sauce that is superb with steamed vegetables, broiled chicken, or fish.

LET US COMPARE LETTUCE

In comparing all but the Stem lettuce, I find that in 100 grams of an edible portion each are pretty equal in food energy, protein, phosphorus, niacin, thiamine, riboflavin, sodium and water content. The Boston, Bibb, and Iceberg have somewhat lower fat content. Iceberg has nearly half the carbohydrate and potassium total of the others. Romaine and Looseleaf have the highest calcium content, while Boston/Bibb has a comparable one half and Iceberg has one third of the calcium content. Boston/Bibb is highest in iron, Romaine and Looseleaf have one quarter less. Iceberg has the lowest iron content with .5 milligrams. Finally, Romaine and Looseleaf have a much greater content of vitamin A and ascorbic acid.

So, if you are splitting hairs there are some differences but all of the lettuce has nutritional value and is the perfect host for wonderful salads of fresh vegetables and fruits.

FRANK'S FACT ON LETTUCE

Store all lettuce away from apples, pears, or tomatoes because ethylene gas emitted from such fruits will cause russet spotting on the lettuce.

Keep your lettuce moisturized by dipping it in water, shaking out excess water, and storing in a plastic bag in the refrigerator crisper.

There is an easy way to put your lettuce in a plastic bag. Simply put your hand into the bag, grab the lettuce in that hand, and turn the bag inside out over the held lettuce!

For lettuce salad so crisp it crackles, try putting it in the freezer for one minute.

SPINACH

Wow, has spinach been around for a long time? Yes, it certainly has. In 1390, a cookbook for the Court of Richard II contained recipes for spynoches. This was the early name for spinach.

In buying spinach, choose bright green leaves and check the bands around the leaves. This will tell you how fresh it is. If the spinach is not fresh, it will be slimy under the band.

When you get it home and want to wash it, remove the bands, put the spinach in salt water to remove the sand, bugs or anything that's on it. Then put it through clear water once or twice to get rid of the salt. Shake out the excess water and store in a plastic bag in your refrigerator's vegetable crisper.

For something healthy, try spinach and lentils. Cook the spinach. Cook the lentils. Put them both together, add vinegar or olive oil (and I don't mean Popeye's girlfriend!)

| A real friend will tell you when you have spinach stuck in your teeth. |

MUSHROOMS

Fresh mushrooms should be stored and refrigerated in a paper bag, or they will become slimy in plastic. When selecting mushrooms, pick them out carefully. When a shopper rubs their hand over all the mushrooms, it brings out the dirt and discolors them.

To clean mushrooms, take out only those that are needed for immediate use. Rinse them in a solution of 1 tablespoon vinegar to 1 quart of water. Just shake them around and they are clean. Pat dry.

Since the stems are as flavorful as the crowns of the mushroom, be sure to use them too. Just take a very small slice from the base of the stem to trim. Also, you may use white wine or lemon juice to keep the mushrooms white in your salad.

Don't use aluminum pans to cook mushrooms as they will turn the pan black.

Mushrooms can be frozen by adding 1/2 teaspoon salt and 1/2 teaspoon lemon juice to 1 quart boiling water. Add the washed mushroom and return to boil. Boil three minutes, rinse mushrooms in cold water, drain, and pat dry. Bag and freeze and they will keep for months.

CHANTERELLE MUSHROOMS have a delicate mushroom flavor and they look like a curving trumpet with small ribs. They are golden orange in color and apricot scented. The chanterelle should be cooked before eating.

They are available from September to April and you can check with the forestry department as to where you can hunt for them in Oregon, Washington, and California.

BLACK CHANTERELLE MUSHROOMS have an earthy flavor, are grayish black in color, and fluted in shape. They should be cooked before eating. They are available in Oregon from January through March.

MOREL MUSHROOM is a wild mushroom which grows primarily in the Pacific Northwest. It resembles a pine cone as its cap has a honeycomb texture and is creamy tan to brown to black in color. The morel has an earthy flavor, but cannot be eaten raw.

The morel should be used in soups, stews, pasta, fish, meat, and poultry dishes. They are available from April to June and again, contact the forestry department about possible hunting grounds.

They are nice people to know.

In all cases, you must have very good knowledge about mushroom before you go out mushroom hunting. I want to remind you that many wild mushroom are deadly if ingested. I hunt for my mushroom in the market and I hope you will too, unless you are a mushroom expert!

ORANGES

The sweet orange in its many varieties is the most extensively grown citrus in the world. Climatic conditions in California makes it possible to cover a twelve month shipping season with two types of oranges — the Washington Navel from Brazil, November to May; and the Valencia from Spain, May to November.

It is necessary to use a larger quantity of oranges in Florida to get through the year. Florida uses the Washington, Hamlin, Pineapple, Parson, and Valencias which are all very juicy and sweet. The biggest use of Florida oranges goes into the making of orange juice.

Texas and Arizona produce oranges also. No matter where they are grown, it is a wonderful piece of fruit. All of the oranges need care from you.

Since citrus does not ripen after harvest, what you see is what you get. Buy heavy fruit that is not puffy on the outside. Learn to buy oranges by the case.

Set them out in the garage, but place the box on top of two blocks of wood or on bricks. Otherwise, the concrete draws moisture into the box and into any oranges in that box.

Put some of your box of oranges into the refrigerator and then eat from the box supply. Leave the paper that you find in a box of oranges. It is treated to prevent spoilage. If your oranges start to go bad on you, wash the good ones and squeeze and freeze the juice.

BLOOD ORANGES

Blood oranges are also called the Moro orange. It is mighty nutritional and fun to eat. It is called the blood orange because of its deep burgundy flesh. When my son, Steve, was in Italy, he ordered a glass of orange juice. When he got it, it looked like tomato juice. But, when he tasted it, it was delightful. The flavor is very distinctive with a hint of raspberry added to the rich orange taste.

In the 1930's, Italian and Spanish immigrants brought blood oranges to America. The moro oranges are native to China. Due to larger interest, planting has increased and more oranges are available now. You will find blood oranges in the markets from mid-December to mid-April.

PEARS

You can't judge a pear by its color. You know that a Bartlett pear, which is a Williams pear in Europe, is ripe when it turns bright yellow. Or, when a Red Bartlett is bright crimson, it is ripe. The winter pears usually don't change color as they ripen.

The Anjou, Bosc, and Comice, as well as Nellis, Seckel, and Forelle pears may not be ripe when you buy them. There is an easy way to tell you if they are ripe. The pear is ripe and ready when it yields to "gentle" pressure at the stem end. When it is ripe, the pear is sweet, buttery, tender, and filled with juice.

Too many shoppers pick pears by squeezing the sides. After four or more shoppers squeeze it, the pear gets soft but not ripe.

Most markets do not leave the pear wrappers on the pear. The wrappers are intended to protect it from stem bruises. When selecting your pears, don't put too many in a single bag. Use two bags so the pears will not bruise by rubbing together.

You may ripen your pears at home by putting them in a brown paper bag. Just squeeze shut the bag and don't refrigerate during ripening.

The Bartlett pear is the pear used commercially for drying. It ripens to a bright yellow and is excellent for fresh eating. It is best for canning because it is juicy and sweet. The Red Bartlett may be used same as the yellow. They are in season from August through December.

The Anjou pear is one of the finest pears, especially if you let it ripen correctly. They are juicy, good keepers and will ship very well. The Anjou season is from October to May.

Want a good baking pear? Try a Bosc. A ripe Bosc has golden brown skin with a network of russeting over golden yellow. The Bosc season runs from August to May.

The Comice pear tends to turn from green to greenish yellow when ripe. The eating quality is superb. The Comice is wonderful for fruit baskets and gift boxes. Its season is from August to March.

Winter Nellis is a medium to small pear. The flesh is creamy and sweet with good eating and cooking qualities. Winter Nellis season runs from October to April.

The Forelle pear is a small winter pear. As it ripens, the Forelle turns a golden yellow and red blush with pronounced freckles. It is sweet and juicy. The season is from October through February.

The Seckel pear is the smallest of all pears in all varieties. Often, the bite-size flesh is a warm light ivory. The Pear Bureau tells me this is the only true pear grown in America. If this fruit was larger, the Seckel would challenge the world as a market for pears. It is widely used as a pear for home orchards.

Many people have pear trees in their back yard and have trouble getting the pears to ripen correctly. They usually end up mushy and soft after they ripen. Once you pick your pears, you must refrigerate them for at least 24 hours. Remove the pears and store in a cool, dry place.

On the West Coast, when the pears are picked they are rushed to the cold rooms to lower the pulp temperature. This lets the pears ripen naturally.

If you want to ripen a box of pears, put newspaper on top of the box without the lid on it. The ethylene gas will do the rest. But remember, once a pear starts to ripen, there is no stopping it.

In the early 1900's, Hood River, Oregon growers suffered a huge freeze. They had been growing 75 percent of their crop as apples. Since that freeze, 75 percent of Hood River's crops are pears. The growers switched to the pear which loves the northwest climate.

A man can have no better epitaph than that which is inscribed in the hearts of his friends.

FRANK'S FACTS ON PEARS

A pear is ripe and ready when it yields to "gentle pressure" at the stem end.

Winter pears usually don't change color as they ripen.

You may ripen pears by putting them is a brown paper bag. Squeeze the bag shut, leaving a small opening.

The Bosc pear is a good baking pear.

The Comice pear is wonderful for fruit baskets and gift boxes. It turns from green to yellow when ripe.

The Seckel pear is the smallest pear, but is most widely used in home orchards.

Refrigerate freshly picked, home orchard pears for at least 24 hours to lower the pulp temperature. This lets the pear ripen from the outside in.

Remember, once a pear starts to ripen, there is no stopping it.

Pears have one ounce of fat and no sodium. They are high in fiber. A medium Bartlett is only 98 calories while a small winter pear has only 61 calories. All are high in potassium.

PINEAPPLE

Not only are pineapple good to eat, they are a sign of hospitality. Many of the English colonists placed carved pineapples over doorways and on gateposts to tell strangers that they were welcome.

Christopher Columbus discovered pineapples growing in the West Indies in 1493. He took some back to Queen Isabella of Spain where they were greatly appreciated. Lucky Queen!

The key to buying a good pineapple is to remember that pineapples do not ripen after they are picked. They are ripe when they are still green outside. The plantations call it "green shell ripe." Make sure that the pineapple has no wet spots or dried out tops or it will be fermenting. Pulling the leaves from the crown to determine the ripeness of a pineapple is an old wives tale and is as valid as kicking the tires of a used car.

Pineapple plants do not grow from seeds, but from slips or from planting the entire crown of leaves. If you want to try planting a pineapple crown, make sure to dry it out for a few days before planting it in a shallow pot. The planting mixture should be one half soil, one quarter humus, and one quarter dried coffee grounds. Just don't be in a hurry as it takes two years for the first crop, 18 months more for a second crop, and 12 months more for a third.

The tough, spiny skin of the pineapple prevents insecticides from getting inside so that all pineapples, organically grown or not, are relatively free from this danger.

To prepare your pineapple, twist the base of green leaves off the top. Then cut off the top and bottom of the fruit. Insert a long, thin boning knife from top to bottom between the outside skin and the fruit. If your knife isn't long enough, cut the pineapple in half again.

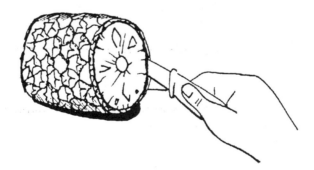

Begin turning the pineapple around the knife until the entire pineapple has been circled. Slide the fruit out of the skin, cut in half lengthwise and slice again. Cut it on a bias or angle, making three cuts on 1/2 of the pineapple.

Put your cut pieces on a plate or tray and squeeze the cut ends and shell over the pineapple pieces. Your cut pineapple will turn instantly sweet! Leave it out exposed to the air for an hour or so, and then refrigerate and it will have a four to five day shelf life.

Many years ago when I was a child my mother used to have ham with a big bone in it for Sunday dinner. I always wondered why she would put a slice of pineapple on top of it while it cooked. I know now that pineapple is a natural tenderizer. I guess Mother knows best!

My first encounter with a fresh pineapple was when I was being inducted into the U.S. Navy at Scofield Barracks, in Hawaii. We were on the Narrow Gage Train traveling three to five miles per hour up a hill through a pineapple field. About ten of us jumped off the train to pick pineapples!

We deserved a blue heart for our wounds because you don't win with the prickly leaves of the pineapple. The Shore Patrol really laughed at us, and the moral of the story is, "Don't grapple with a pineapple. It will win!"

FRANK'S FACTS ON PINEAPPLE

Pineapples do not continue to ripen after they are picked.

In choosing a pineapple, make sure that it has no wet spots or dried out tops which are signs of fermenting.

The tough, spiny skin of the pineapple prevents insecticides from getting inside the pineapple.

Pineapple plants do not grow from seeds, but from slips or from planting the entire crown of leaves.

Pineapple is a natural tenderizer.

TOMATO

Is it, or isn't it? A tomato is a vegetable only because in 1893 it was made into a vegetable by an Act of Congress. Actually it is a fruit, but because of the way we use it, it is call a vegetable. Confused? So am I. The botanical answer to this debate is that it is neither a vegetable or fruit! It is a berry. A berry is defined as any fleshy, simple fruit with one or more seeds and a skin. The tomato is a berry — being pulpy and containing one or more seeds that are not stones.

The tomato has been called the apple of the Moors, the golden apple, and the love apple. I asked my Dad about the name love apple. He laughed and said, "In Italy they had big, big pots to cook the tomatoes for sauce. These pots needed some one to keep the fires going. The older people went to bed, leaving the younger to keep the logs on the fire." Hmmmmm, so the name love apple was named for this system, according to Dad, and that's enough said!

Everyone has different ideas of how a tomato should taste. People want it to taste as if it was just picked out of their garden. So, this one item causes the produce person the most grief. I have seen shoppers choose beautiful, ripe tomatoes, put them in a bag and then place groceries on top of them. Please give them as much care as you have in selecting them.

If you buy tomatoes from a store that has them under refrigeration, you will find that when you use them they will be watery because the cold has broken down the tomato cells. Because they have already been refrigerated, it is necessary to keep them refrigerated.

Actually, no tomato should be refrigerated unless it is really ripe. Tomatoes (we know now!) are a fruit so if you don't put your green bananas in the refrigerator to ripen, then don't expect your tomatoes to ripen in there either.

Grandma used to ripen tomatoes by putting them on the window sill. Our homes today have different glass which causes the tomato to cook in the afternoon sun, and freeze in the evening. This hot and cold process is not good. They are better off in a bowl on the drain board, but the very best place to ripen your tomatoes is on TOP of your refrigerator, not in it. There is even heat up there and imagine how beautiful they will look up there as they ripen!

If you have a garden, pick your tomatoes in the heat of the day. Your tomato will taste better. If your tomato crop gets away from you, instead of just eating them or giving some to your neighbors, try turning them into sauce you can freeze for later use. The Home Canning book by Sunset has a wonderful Tomato Sauce recipe.

One of the best sauce tomatoes is the ROMA TOMATO. It has a lot of vine-ripened flavor and it cooks down to a nice color sauce. Roma tomatoes have a high amount of solid matter and ripens over a short period of time. Keep tomatoes in a warm spot to ripen faster.

CHERRY TOMATOES can be planted in a very small area, or even a container. The plant will repay you with more tomatoes than you can eat. Cherry tomatoes can be a heavy producer with loving care, and they go well on vegetable trays or just eating out of hand.

I have been eating tomatoes that I picked in October during January. And they taste wonderful. This is my method...

Pick tomatoes that have been in the garden when frost is predicted. Separate those showing red from the full green ones. Pack green tomatoes by wrapping each one with pear wrappers (remember when I told you to save the pear wrappers in the December chapter on holiday baskets?) or newspaper. Place the wrapped green tomatoes, not more than six tomatoes deep, in an orange or apple box with a lid.

Complete this same process for the tomatoes showing red color, but place them in a separate box because they will ripen quicker. Mature, green tomatoes will ripen with this method in about two weeks, at 65-75 degree room temperature. You may slow down the ripening by storing the box at 55 degrees causing the tomatoes to ripen in about one month. If you store your vegetables and fruit in a basement that has a furnace, insulate and partition an area to keep cooler.

Another method for ripening green tomatoes...

Before the first frost, pull up the tomato (vine, roots and all) and put a plastic bag over the roots as soon as possible. Otherwise, the air will get to the roots and dry them. Next, hang the plants in the garage or cool basement. I would suggest you could put netting or a large plastic bag around the tomatoes so the gases will be kept in. Tie it off with a pipe cleaner so you can still get to the tomatoes when they've ripened. You will smell the ripeness and see the red color of the tomato when they are ready to enjoy. And you will be amazed?

Several kinds of vegetables from the garden can continue to be enjoyed when frost puts an end to the season outdoors by using proper storage and ripening processes.

FRANK'S FACTS ON TOMATOES

Tomatoes are called vegetables by an Act of Congress. It is actually a berry.

No tomato should be refrigerated unless it is really ripe.

Put unripe tomatoes on top of your refrigerator to ripen because there is even heat up there.

Just remember, a tomato ripens from inside out and if you don't let them ripen by heat and moisture, they will not have any flavor.

Before 1960, root vegetables were popular. Beets, turnips, carrots, onions, and potatoes to name a few. After 1960, restaurants seem to have forgotten that root vegetables even existed. The roots lost out to farmers who were growing broccoli, asparagus, lettuce, artichokes, and even tomatoes.

But, what goes around comes around, and in the 1990's roots are being dressed up again by chefs in the finest restaurants around. They have rediscovered that roots are tasty and good for you. This spring, plant some roots in your garden. I know people who keep them in the ground all winter by mulching over them with straw or plastic. It surely "beets" going to the store for them!

FRANK'S FACTS ON ROOT VEGETABLES

Remember my mother's cooking rule: if it grows under the ground, wash with cold water, start cooking with cold water, and cover pot with a lid. If it grows above ground, it grows in hot sun uncovered. So, start it in boiling water with no lid.

Turnips & Rutabaga

Have you ever wondered what people ate before potatoes? In Europe they had the Swedish turnip; today we call it a rutabaga. It was a staple for them, good keepers, and easy to grow. Rutabagas are high in vitamin C and minerals and are available all year long. However, turnips and rutabaga are two different vegetables. Turnips are round roots with purple-tinted, white skin. Rutabaga are round with light yellow-brown skin, and yellow flesh.

Both should be firm and heavy for their size. Each have a special taste of their own. Both of them can be prepared in the same way: mashed, boiled, shredded, and baked. They add flavor and nutrients to soups and stews. Sometimes the rutabaga is waxed to preserve it for longer shelf life. In any case, make sure you peel both the turnip and rutabaga.

Carrots

We have come a long way since the day that carrot tops were worn in the hair as a garland. It looked like Queen Ann Lace.

Before 1951, nearly all carrots sold fresh were sold with tops intact. It was a beautiful sight and one that has stayed with me through the years. Seeing farmers with carrots packed on flat bed trucks, taking them to market was a sight to see. They were not in boxes, but they were loose and piled five feet high — 10 feet long. Most farmers packed them in bunches of six. Beets and turnips were packed the same way. The truck was a beautiful thing to see.

Now, researchers have learned that the carrot tops draw moisture from the roots and this hastens shriveling. Within a few years, nearly all carrots were marketed as topped and prepacked.

Look for bright colored carrots when buying them. Carrots are one of the best sources of vitamin A, and raw carrots are rich in carotene. Fresh carrots are a rich source of vitamin C and a good source of fiber and potassium, too.

Many people like to juice their carrots. An eight ounce glass provides 40,000 to 50,000 units of vitamin C. Remember, too much carrot juice will turn your skin orange but it will return to your natural shade if you stop drinking it for awhile!

When I was in La Mont, California, I went through the Bugs Bunny plant there. We all may think that the carrot fields are all around the plant, right? Wrong.

The carrot fields are as far away as 100-150 miles. When I saw the open dump trucks bringing in the carrots after three or four hours in the hot sun, they looked terrible. They were all soft and wilted. The dump truck loaded the carrots onto a conveyor containing water. The cold water was used to reduce the temperature of the carrots while they were washed.

The pulp temperature of the carrot can be hydrocooled for 70 to 40 degrees F. in nine minutes. Mechanical refrigeration was used to cool the water for this operation. I could not believe how lowering the pulp temperature could make so much difference.

When you have carrots that are soft or carrots freshly picked from your garden, put them in ice cold water for 15 minutes. They will keep fresher longer.

Fresh carrots are wonderful when cooked to a crisp tenderness. They are added to soups and stews, and may be served as a side-dish, too. Make carrot cake. Carrots must be good for your eyes because I have never seen a rabbit wearing a pair of glasses!

Parsnips

Parsnips resemble carrots in shape, but are cream or tan in color. They should be well formed, smooth, and firm. Their nutty flavor can be enjoyed fried, boiled, and served with cream sauce.

Parsnips are wonderful when simmered in stews, and they are best cooked by blanching first. Just boil covered for 20 minutes until tender, then cool and remove the skins.

Parsnips are high in potassium, low in calorie, and a good source of fiber.

Plant parsnips in your garden. Leave them in the ground during the winter. The cool weather makes them sweeter. It turns the starch to sugar. Before the potato was discovered, the parsnip was a staple along with the rutabaga and turnip.

Radishes

To store fresh radishes and keep them fresh, try this technique. Wash the radishes, slice off the tops, and while they are still damp from the washing put them in a covered jar in the refrigerator. If you didn't put a lid on the jar it would cause too much moisture in the refrigerator. Think about dicing the tops of the radishes and add to a salad for a semi-bitter flavor. It will combine with your choice of salad dressing!

Beets

Try choosing beets with fresh looking tops. That is one way to get two vegetables for the price of one. The tops may be washed and cooked just as you would spinach.

Make sure you leave an inch or so of leaves on the beets. They will not bleed red when you cook them, and will keep their color. You can also add a little vinegar to the water to retain their color. And, peel your beets after you have cooked them. The skins slip right off. Really...try it!

Beets are low in calories and good food for your blood. The greens are high in vitamin A and iron. Fresh beets are a wonderful meal accompaniment. Their fresh cooked flavor and ruby-red color are delightful and great in salads, added to soups, baked or fried, and pickled. Try the golden beet for a special treat.

PRODUCE FROM AROUND THE WORLD

Isn't it funny how names tend to confuse the shoppers. Names like Mo Qua — Bitter Melon — Tamarind — Opo — Jerusalem Artichokes — Kabocha — Scallion — Salsify — Fennel — Chayote — Cherimoya — Jicama — Kiwana — Malanga — I could go on and on — how about Passion Fruit ?!?

We can buy any of these unusual items in a store. In other countries we must remember that the harvest is only what the land offers. Many of these items have been brought to the United States from Asia, South America, and other parts of the world.

ROOTS OF THE WORLD

Ginger Root

The Ginger Root comes from the Fuji Islands between July to December, and from the Hawaiian Islands from November to May. It is the root of the ginger plant.

I have four ways to keep ginger — plant it, buy what you need, freeze it (but you must grate more than you need and it seems to lose some of its flavor), and my favorite of putting it in a jar of sherry with a lid. It will keep indefinitely. It also picks up the flavor of the sherry which is wonderful for oriental cooking.

Jerusalem Artichoke

It is called a Jerusalem Artichoke but only has the name of artichoke and is no relation at all. It also is called Sunchokes because it is of sunflower plant origin.

Sunchokes have a flavor similar to the globe artichoke. This root vegetable has a knobby appearance and nutty taste. Use it the same as you would use water chestnuts. It adds extra crunch to salads with sliced, raw sun chokes. Or serve them boiled, sauteed, or mashed. A sunchoke has no starch, but it is very crunchy. It will discolor quickly after being cut, so soak pieces in water to which vinegar has been added until ready to use.

Here is a little tip from me. I gave my brother-in-law five pounds of sun chokes to plant in Talbert, Oregon. He had a large garden and harvested at least 40 pounds out of the planting. The only trouble was that for the next five years, they were coming up all throughout his garden and grass. We laughed about it while I was on my knees pulling up the roots.

Jicama

Jicama (HEE-ka mah) is called a yam bean or Fon Goot. In Mexico it is a common root vegetable. It resembles a turnip and is a white tuber with a brown stringy covering that is easily peeled.

A dash of lime or lemon really brings out the sweet flavor. It can be used same as water chestnuts in soups, salads, or stews. It can be steamed, boiled, sauteed, or stir-fried, but best of all can be eaten raw. Jicama stays crisp when cooked and does not darken as fast as potatoes.

Kohlrabi

Kohlrabi (call RAH-bee) in a word means cabbage turnip. The globular bulb has a delicate turnip-like taste. And, again, we have two vegetables in one.

The tops can be cooked like any fresh greens. Strip the stems just before using. Wash, peel, and cut in strips for dipping or add to stir-fry combinations. To cook bulb, quarter it and steam in lightly salted water until crisp and tender. Drain, season with fresh lemon or lime juice.

Malanga

There are over 40 species of Malanga, all native to the American tropics. This root has yellow or reddish flesh and the interior may be cream, yellow, or reddish. It has a crisp, slippery texture and cooked Malanga is one of the love or hate foods.

Its taste tends more toward nuts instead of potatoes. In most countries, malanga is peeled and boiled. It is used with sausage, dried meat, and fish dishes. To cook it you boil the peeled malanga (having cut it into potato size pieces) in salted water for 20-25 minutes. Malanga also makes ideal chips. Sprinkle with chili powder, to taste.

Salsify

Salsify is sometimes called Oyster plant because of flavor similar to oysters. This root resembles parsnip, with heavy, grassy tops. The roots are gray-white in color with firm, juicy flesh.

Salsify discolors when cut, so cook immediately after preparing. Place in boiling, salted water to which one teaspoon vinegar has been added for each inch of water. Cook 5-10 minutes. Drain and season with salt, pepper, and butter. When cooked, it is wonderful in European cooking and in soups.

Scallions

Scallions are young onion bulbs picked before the bulb matures. If it did get bigger it would be a dry onion. Scallions is the name in the eastern U.S.; in the west, scallions are called green onions.

Taro Root

The Taro Root is well known in Hawaii. Taro is eaten mostly in the form of poi. The starch grains in taro are the smallest in any plant. It makes them readily digestible.

It can be baked, steamed, boiled or used in soup as potatoes. It has a bland, starchy taste with the texture of a potato.

They are extremely nutritious and in 100 grams, it offers a good amount of calcium, phosphorus, iron, potassium, vitamin A, vitamin C, plus other minerals and vitamins.

Again, this is something you like or don't like. When I had poi in Hawaii, I was one of those that didn't like. Sorry.

Yucca Root

The Yucca Root is known as cassava. It is a large starchy root. It is also called Manioc and the starch derived from the root of the plant is used to make tapioca.

It is a staple food in the tropics and is used the same as a potato. It is shaped like a elongated sweet potato with pink to brown skin and white flesh.

FRUIT & VEGETABLES OF THE WORLD

Bitter Melon

Bitter Melon, also known as Foo Gwa, is about the size of a cucumber and has silvery green flesh with red seeds inside. The skin is edible, but the seeds should be removed.

It is a member of the squash family and has a taste similar to bland squash, but more sour. Soaking bitter melon in salt water will remove the bitterness. It may be stuffed, cooked or steamed, curried, or pickled.

Bok Choy

Bok Choy is also called Chinese Chard. This vegetable has broad white or greenish white stalks with loose dark green leaves. Select fresh, crisp, firm heads. Store unwashed in a plastic bag in the refrigerator and use within a few days.

To prepare, cut off the root ends. Separate stalks and remove tough or wilted leaves. Cut leaves from stem and slice in one inch pieces. Slice stems diagonally in thick pieces.

Bok Choy is a sweet and mild-tasting vegetable that can be stir-fried, or served raw in salads. Try the baby bok choy for stir-frying, also.

Breadfruit

Breadfruit looks like a pineapple that grows on a tree. It is used as a vegetable.

It was the cargo which Captain Bly of the Bounty carried when he had the mutiny, and again on his next attempt to sail to Tahiti. He was taking breadfruit to Tahiti so it could be grown as food for the Chinese workers.

Prepare breadfruit as you would potatoes by slicing, deepfrying, or boiling. It has the texture of bread when cooked. Breadfruit is a food staple of Polynesia. It also grows in Central and South America, and Mexico.

Chayote

Chayote (chy-O-tay) is called a Vegetable-Pear. The fruit is round to pear shaped. The surface is covered with small, soft spines. It is more delectable than squash in flavor.

Creole cooks call it Mirliton. South American cooks call it mango squash. People in Florida, where it is a main vegetable, call it the Vegetable-Pear.

I have been told that as many as 60 chayotes grow on one vine. It is grown successfully in California. It is one of the most versatile of all fresh vegetables.

Chayote is very popular in Cuba, Mexico, and Florida. Although it looks like a pear, it is a squash. When young it has no pit and is very tender.

Chayotes flavor is a cross between an apple and a cucumber. Use it as a vegetable — steamed, baked, stuffed, or fried. It is used in salads, main dishes, and desserts. The green or white skin can be peeled like an apple.

Cherimoya

Cherimoya (chair-ih-MO-ya) was prized by the Incas. This delicious subtropical fruit has grown in California for over 100 years. California now produces enough quantity that you may discover this rare and exotic fruit for yourself.

The cherimoya is sweet and juicy, with a creamy custard-like texture. It tastes like papaya, pineapple, and banana. In midsummer when the tree blooms, each flower must be pollinated by hand to ensure a crop.

Select fruit which is firm and light yellowish in color. Ripen at room temperature. Cherimoya tastes best when chilled and it will taste like custard. Squeeze a little orange juice over it to enhance the flavor.

Cherimoya blends well with most varieties of fruit and compotoes (a fruit stewed with sugar)!

Fennel

Fennel (or Anise or Finocchio, as the Italians call it) is a large bulb that tastes like licorice.

Sprinkle the lacy leaves over fish, put the stalks in many Italian dishes, or serve the bulb raw as a vegetable. After cooking, the flavor changes and it is also used on relish dishes. Do not confuse this with Anise seeds. Try fennel in any dish where you would use celery, but would like a new, unique flavor.

Kabocha

Kabocha (kah-BAH-chee) is an asian pumpkin. The flesh is deep orange and is a wonderful keeper. Use it the same as winter squash, and it is delicious baked with brown sugar. Steamed, boiled — try it, you will enjoy it.

Kiwano

Kiwano (kee-WAH-no) is a new fruit to us, but has been known for over 3,000 years. This African horned melon is oblong shaped and can reach 4-6 inches in length.

It has the flavor of lime, bananas, and cucumber. It is golden orange colored when ripe and is distinctive because of its spikes. The Kiwano has white seeds encased in juicy green pulp with a jelly-like texture.

Lychee Nut

The Lychee Nut is vastly popular in Asia and has been for 2,000 years. The matured fruit looks like an overgrown strawberry. In flavor, it is suggestive of a Royal Ann Cherry.

The fruit can be stored for two to three weeks without losing its flavor. It is now grown in Jamaica, Hawaii, Brazil, Florida, and California. The best place to look for the lychee nut is in an asian market.

Mo Qua

Mo Qua is a form of summer squash. It has small fuzz on it and is sometimes called Hairy Squash. You would use it the same as zucchini.

Okra

Okra is another vegetable that you may love or not. It is highly perishable and hard to handle. Okra needs high humidity, but not full water. Sprinkling it will cause it to get slimy. Long exposure will cause it to blacken.

Okra does add zip to soups. It is used heavily in New Orleans Creole cooking where okra is called gumbo. It is best to buy pods — 3 to 4 inches long.

Opo

Opo is just another squash cooked the same as zucchini. It is very good in soup or stews and is very flavorable.

Passion Fruit or Grandilla

Passion Fruit is the edible fruit of the passion flower. It is the size and shape of a large egg, with a tough purple skin, yellow flesh, and many black, edible seeds. It is generally eaten in the fresh stage with a spoon. Passion fruit is also used in cakes, jellies, or made into a beverage. It has a sweet, acid flavor.

Rhubarb

Well, here we go again. Botanically, rhubarb is a vegetable, however in use it is considered a fruit. On July 17, 1947 the U.S. Customs Court at Buffalo, New York ruled that rhubarb is a fruit and not a vegetable.

This is important... only the leafstalk of rhubarb is good to eat. The leaf blade should never be eaten. The leaf has a high content of oxalic acid and can be quite harmful. In the stalks, it is harmless.

Rhubarb is used as a fruit because of its high acidity and flavor. It has long been popular in pies and is referred as a pie plant. Rhubarb wilts at room temperature. It should be kept cold. Put moisture on it before refrigeration to keep it fresh.

Tamarinds

Tamarinds is a flat, cinnamon colored pod. The fruit is very acidic. It is used to make ice cold drinks, but the main use is in Worcestershire Sauce.

Wing Beans

Wing Beans are long, edible pods tasting like a cross between a french string bean and a snow pea. The Wing Bean is not exactly a household word in the U.S. It is very sensitive to the cold and in 1975 it was grown only in New Guinea and Southeast Asia. Since 1975, it has been planted in 70 more countries. It has become one of the items being used to feed the world's hungry. Wing Beans are very bountiful and grows like a weed. It produces shoots, leaves, flowers, tubers, pods, seeds, and a cooking oil that are all tasty, nutritious, and high in protein. They are also disease resistant, high-yielding, and quick growing — but only in the tropics.

Each bean has four ruffled, equally spaced wings or fins that run its length. Steam them whole and then saute in butter with chopped parsley and garlic. Or, slice crosswise and stir-fry the four-sided slices and sprinkle with black sesame seeds.

FRANK'S FAVORITE TOOLS FOR PRODUCE

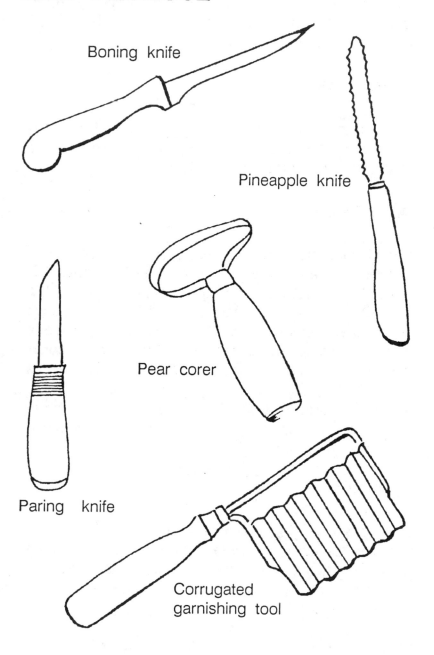

Boning knife

Pineapple knife

Pear corer

Paring knife

Corrugated
garnishing tool

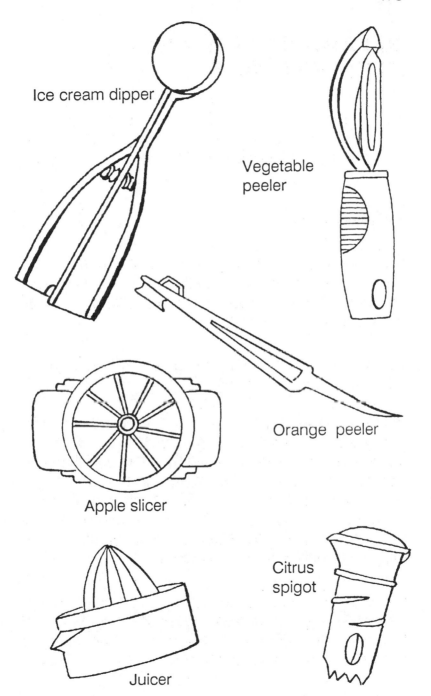

Ice cream dipper

Vegetable peeler

Orange peeler

Apple slicer

Juicer

Citrus spigot

REFRIGERATION AND ETHELYNE GAS

Two processes, one man-made and one natural, have helped the produce industry join the jet age. One stops the ripening process and the other accelerates it. The first is refrigeration, and the second is ethylene gas.

Refrigeration

Ok, what is a refrigerator? It is nothing more than a holding box. You put items in it to keep them at a certain temperature. Cold is a non-conductor of heat. Items will not ripen in refrigeration.

So why do customers put green melons, green tomatoes, green bananas in the refrigerator and wonder why they don't taste better when they use them? Well, what you have done is lower the pulp temperature of the fruit. It will never ripen right. No fruit that needs ripening should be put in until it is ripe. For instance, bananas can be put in the refrigerator only at the ripeness you desire. Tomatoes will turn watery if you put them in the refrigerator when they are not ripe first. Remember, put a tomato in the refrigerator only after it is ripened.

Hydro-cooling and vacuum-cooling are processes the packing plants use to lower the pulp temperature of fruit and vegetables in order to stop the ripening process. Temperature-controlled refrigerated trucks allow some cargo that is already ripe to arrive at our markets still fresh and ready to enjoy.

Refrigeration has come a long way from the days of stacking iceberg lettuce on layers of ice for delivery.

Ethylene Gas

What is ethylene gas? It is a colorless gas with a sweet, ether-like odor. It is clear that ethylene is a ripening hormone. It is a chemical substance produced by fruits that accelerates the normal process of ripening.

Ethylene gas is not harmful to human health. In fact, it was used as an anesthetic in hospitals for years, until a less flammable compound was developed.

Growers start the ripening process of fruit with one part of ethylene gas to over a million parts of air. Ethylene gas helps the natural ripening of fruit and is used to speed the ripening process when necessary.

You can smell ethylene gas when you have an over-ripe apple and it gives an odor. It is harmless, of course.

If you never stick your neck out, you'll never get your head above the crowd.

Tips for a Smart Produce Shopper

1. Eat better by buying smarter.

2. Take time to shop and don't be afraid to ask questions. You need time to find the best bargains. If something is not as good as it was advertised, take it back.

3. Be adventurous, experiment with new varieties of fruits and vegetables, whatever is unusual and in season. Experiment with new ingredients in salads, like raisins, raw yams, or daikon.

4. Use the words "fruit and vegetables" on your shopping list rather than being specific. See what looks good and is the best buy. Don't let your shopping list box you into an expensive corner.

5. Try to make the grocery store your last stop so your purchases don't sit in the car too long.

6. Put fruit and vegetables in your sack lunches. If possible, cut it up ahead and put the ready-to-eat items in ziplock bags.

7. Check into case pricing of oranges, apples, etc. If you find a large saving, share with a friend or neighbor who is interested in a good deal.

8. Plan menus with an eye to what is in season.

9. Figure your cost per serving, it will be an indication of value. For example, a watermelon at 49 cents a pound will serve many compared to strawberries at 39 cents per basket that will serve fewer.

10. After you get home, take the time to put your perishables away properly. Remove any rubberband or twist-tie from your produce. The time spent can improve the life of your purchases.

11. Make your meals a time for togetherness. Use the time when you sit at the table to enjoy not only the food, but each other. Please turn off the TV and talk.

PRODUCE MAN TO PRODUCE MERCHANDISER

There have been many changes in the produce industry with new varieties, prepackaging of produce, nutritious value of items, ad shoppers, etc. — all of the above are major changes from just two or three years ago.

A produce man, or should I say produce person, has to be able to understand what has taken place. A salesman has become a salesperson who is called a market associate. Personnel is now called Human Resources. A produce buyer is now a produce merchandiser but, even with all of these changes a customer is still a customer.

What is a customer? The dictionary says a customer is one who trades regularly at a particular shop, a patron, a purchaser or buyer. Now we know what a customer is, then how do we attract one, keep one and what can you offer one?

Everybody has lettuce, tomatoes, celery so what makes yours better? Sure, you have the best looking produce in town. Not an item out of place. Your prices aren't too high, but it seems like customers are not picking up as many items as you would like. What do you do? Sit on a rock? (I'll explain that later).

Look over what you are trying to accomplish. Put yourself in a customers place. Try to decide what the new items are while looking for the best value. Ask yourself, "What should I buy and what do I do with it?" Your customer will look for someone to ask what is good and what is in season. Be that someone to talk to and give the customer what it takes to make them a regular shopper in your store. Many stores advertise to get a customer in the shop, and then forget that a friendly hello will bring them back. Marketing research says a customer will spend 15 to 25 percent more money in a store that is fun and exciting! And 98 percent of a recent poll indicated that the top reason for choosing a particular supermarket is the quality of produce!

"Sit on a rock," I said because 30 years ago I drove from Portland over Mt. Hood to Bend, Oregon delivering produce that I bought in Portland and sold in Central Oregon. When I was empty and going back to Portland, I would buy twelve tons of potatoes. One thing I didn't carry was a spare tire. I had one in Portland and one in Madras, Oregon. A tire on the tire rack would collect too much snow. Coming across the Warm Springs flats about 60 miles from Madras and 60 miles from Portland, I blew a front tire on my six wheeler. While waiting for a ride, I sat on a big rock and was feeling glum. Then, looking at the truck I started to laugh at how easy my solution was.

Here I was with a flat tire on the front of a truck that had one flat and nine tires. I took one tire off the back and put it on the front and away I went. Good thing I decided to sit on that rock and not in the cab. Today you don't have to sit on a rock, just take the time to think and then act. I am still surprised at how many good decisions I have made since I sat on a rock!

Frank's Top 15 Tips for Produce Marketers:

1. Keep a positive attitude towards the customer.

2. Rotate product as you fill the department.

3. Give service.

4. Don't over-buy on perishable foods, use five or six instead of ten.

5. The wet rack should look as good at 8:00 p.m. as it does at 8:00 a.m.

6. Check your orders. Sometimes an item like bananas might come in riper than the ones you have on hand. Therefore they need to be used first.

7. If prices change, make sure the new prices get processed properly.

8. Work with other departments to help with spoilage. Some items that can be used are potatoes, small leaf items, and celery.

9. Use demonstrators to promote new products. Make sure they know the item they are promoting.

10. Educate your employees as to the uses of fruits and vegetables so they can answer the customer

questions. Have reference material available so answers are handy.

11. Cater to singles and senior citizens. Many of them need smaller portions such as a 1/2 head of cabbage, etc.

12. Listen to people, make each customer feel they are important.

13. Learn how to work and talk at the same time.

14. Use your eyes instead of your legs.

15. Enjoy what you do!

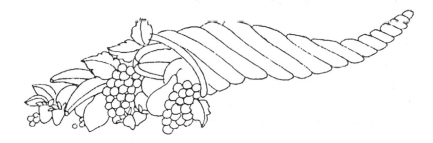

If you think education is expensive, try ignorance.

When a happy person enters the room it is like another candle has been lighted.

THE PRODUCE MAN

Our first produce man is a bit of a freak,
His apron's not white, but his shirt was, last week.
Never heard of a system, just get the stuff out.
"Now what does that sign say?" There seems to be doubt.
"Oh well, what's the difference — they have to buy here,
There isn't another place anywhere near."
He forgets the old adage, about dying and taxes,
And as they pass by, he smokes and relaxes.

Out with the white gloves — here comes number two
He's getting the idea, but yet — what will he do?
At keeping things clean, he has quite a knack,
There's only one thing — people don't buy the rack.
They start for his section, they want to be sold,
But the neat, empty cases are leaving them cold.
They glance here and there — perhaps there's a shortage
Our boy is no help in paying the mortgage.

Well now, lookee here, things are taking a turn
Quite a bit for the better, as soon you will learn.
Number three is a thinker, know what people demand,
And he makes it his business to have it on hand.
He works like a beaver, keeps up quite a pace.
Keeps everything full and always in place.
His shoppers are happy them came to this store,
And depart with the lettuce that they came in for.

Get out extra carts, you know the direction,
To our man number four, and his produce selection.
Lettuce, rows crisp and green; corn, yellow for pickin;
Bright fruits in their baskets to make taste buds quicken.
Cheery rows of tomatoes, cucumbers and beans,

Gold oranges and grapes and sweet nectarines.
This lad is a smart one, this much has been told,
He knows people buy, but they want to be sold.

The sales that we're after, and so often we've missed,
Is the smart modern shopper, armed with a list.
She knows what she wants and she heads for that section.
But see what she does when she see this selection?
Her list is forgotten; she's lost in a dream,
Of a crispy green salad, a fresh soup tureen.
So no — there's a cart, when she'd planned on a sack,
And a satisfied customer, bound to be back.

Author unknown

Makes Friends by Service Slogan reads the
headline from The Oregonian, 1933.

Photo caption:

A section of the modern fruit and vegetable store operated by Joe Candioto, and his wife and son the Grand Central Public Market, SE Ninth Avenue, and Morrison Street. Candioto has been selling home-grown vegetables and fruits since the Grand Central market opened nearly five years ago. His customers have grown steadily. Shown in the picture, from left: Frankie Comella, who is learning the business; Joe Candioto (Frank's uncle) and Mrs. Candioto.

The Frank Comella Story

By Betty Comella

Frank was born in Portland, Oregon in 1920. His parents immigrated from Italy, through Ellis Island in New York. They met and settled in southeast Portland in the early 1900's. It was a neighborhood, mostly Italian, centered around St. Philip Neri Catholic Church.

Frank was the youngest son in a family of four boys and three girls. There were lots of aunts and uncles and cousins close by. His father farmed and had a huge garden to feed the family. In those days, there were plenty of empty lots that were put to good use brimming full of fruits and vegetables all year. The bounty was bartered for other things they needed.

Fruit trees were plentiful. The old apple and cherry trees in those days were huge, not like the dwarf varieties we see today. Most people had a fig tree somewhere in their yard. Everything was eaten, canned, or dried for winter. The days of the horse and buggy were gone, but cars were expensive and a luxury. The Comella family either took the streetcar or walked.

It was a simple way of life. They had no supermarkets, just the small corner store with the owners living in the back. Frank's mother would take the streetcar downtown and buy her food at the open air markets on Yamhill Street, or in Meier & Frank's basement, when it was locally owned. Yes, even M&F was in the food business then. Frank spent his younger years doing anything to help out the family.

Times were hard during the depression. He worked after school at the Grand Central Market on 8th and SE Morrison at his cousin's fruit stand. Then on to working on the produce delivery trucks that went from the Farmers Market to the stores. Frank was always working with produce. Frank's older brothers Lawrence, Joe, and Vince all worked in the produce business one way or another. In the late 30's Frank worked for his brother Lawrence, who leased the produce department at 36th & Hawthorne Street Fred Meyer store. It was one of Fred Meyer's early stores when they were still small. Frank remembers Mr. Meyers and his wife, Eve, coming into the store quite often. Mrs. Meyers always stopped and admired the window displays Frank made.

The only time Frank took time off from produce was during World War II when he was in the Navy. He spent four years as a shipfitter, repairing ships at Pearl Harbor, Hawaii. After the war was over, he returned to Portland. Very soon, he met his future wife, Betty and they were married in September of 1946.

It wasn't long before Frank owned his own truck and started a wholesale route delivering produce to Central Oregon. It was a 30 year experience. He watched the area grow, from Sunriver to Kah-nee-tah, Frank serviced them all. In the meantime, life went on at home. Soon the family grew — first came Sandra, then Stephen, and then Cindy. As the children grew older, Frank became involved in their activities. He became the "pumpkin man" at the elementary school across the street, after giving the 1st graders pumpkins for many years.

It was always a family business. I did the bookkeeping, with the children helping as soon as they were able. There was always something going on in the family garage. If it wasn't making Christmas baskets, it was bagging potatoes.

In 1974, an opportunity came to get off the road and it was a welcome chance for a change. John Hudson offered to lease the produce department at Angelo's in Progress, and Frank was back in retail as though he had never left 40 years before. He gave service, talked to customers, and gave samples like business was run years ago. This was a novel concept in the 70's. He loved it and it showed.

In 1978, Frank, son Steve, and I bought our own store and Comella & Son was opened. After Cindy joined the business, it was renamed Comella & Son & Daughter. The store grew and grew and grew with three enlargements, but the original concepts were always upheld. Fresh fruits and vegetables were once again becoming popular. Customers didn't know how to pick or store them. Radio Station KYXI asked Frank to talk about his favorite subject — produce — on the radio airwaves. And that was the beginning of produce classes, radio, and various local television appearances. He soon became a familiar face in Portland.

Produce was a labor of love for Frank and he never stopped learning about his favorite subject. Whether in the growing fields or in books, he was researching. Frank could always find something to see on a vacation, be it the pineapple fields in Hawaii, or the melon fields in California, sugar bananas in Tahiti, or cherries in Washington.

In 1992, at the age of 72, he was talked into retirement by his family. He needed to slow down. The store was sold, but Frank was soon bored. How many bird houses can a person make?

The produce that runs in Frank's veins wouldn't allow him to stay retired for long. Today you can find him holding court in son Steves store "Comella's Greengrocer," handing out advice and samples just like in the good old days.

Frank also continues to talk produce any chance he gets at convention seminars, hospital health fairs, or at the neighborhood grocery. He writes a monthly column for the Multnomah Village Post newspaper. And he has finally written the book you have in your hands; the book everyone has hoped he would. With Betty's encouragement and that of his family, Frank has left this legacy of his knowledge and a piece of his big heart to share for always.

USDA Food Group Pyramid

HOW MANY SERVINGS DO YOU NEED DAILY? Use these ranges as your guide for how much food to eat each day. Young children (under 5 yrs.) one serving is generally 1/4 - 1/3 of an adult serving.

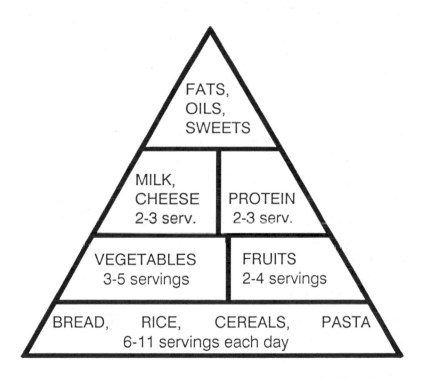

FATS, OILS, SWEETS

MILK, CHEESE 2-3 serv.

PROTEIN 2-3 serv.

VEGETABLES 3-5 servings

FRUITS 2-4 servings

BREAD, RICE, CEREALS, PASTA
6-11 servings each day

VEGETABLES - One serving is: 1/2 cup cooked vegetables, or 1/2 cup raw chopped vegetables, or 1 cup raw leafy vegetables, or 1/2-3/4 cup of juice.

FRUITS - One serving is: 1 whole medium fruit (about 1 cup), or 1/2 cup canned fruit, or 1/4 cup dried fruit, or 1/2-3/4 cup juice.